For Bob Proctor

You taught me to spread love everywhere I go
by spreading love everywhere you went.
You are the magic in this story of hope.

Sandy

CHAPTER ONE
Results

"Where did the time go?" Chloe mused, staring out the window of her cozy cottage. Had it really been six months since her life transformed? It felt like both an eternity and a blink.

On the one hand, her dreams were finally coming true. Her first book, *Sunset at Whisper Creek*, had not only been accepted by her publisher, Multmountain Press, but expanded into a trilogy. Her career had blossomed from stagnant reporter to successful freelance writer and novelist practically overnight. And now here she sat, in a charming cottage behind a stately Pasadena home. No more dreary apartment in Pacoima.

Yet doubts still lingered. Was she truly capable of meeting the high expectations set for her next books? Could she repeat the magic that had brought her here? Try as she might, doubt was a stubborn companion she had yet to be rid of.

But then she remembered Sarah, who saw in her what Chloe herself could not. Their serendipitous meeting six months prior had been the catalyst for Chloe's transformation. Covering Sarah's Unstuck conference, coupled with a heartwarming piece about a local high school football team, had propelled Chloe into the limelight.

She gazed at the arroyo below her window, taking in the beautiful trees and singing birds. The fog of June gloom still lingered, but soon sunny days would return. And with them, Chloe would dive into life anew—starting with morning swims at the Rose Bowl pool down the hill.

The past six months had flown by in a whirlwind, and the next held infinite promise. As long as she could silence her doubts and nurture her dreams, this was just the beginning.

Just then, her cell phone rang. She smiled when she saw the caller's name.

"Sarah!" Chloe said. "I was just thinking about you."

"Great minds think alike, my friend. You've been on my mind, too. How are you doing?"

"Oh, pretty well. I mean, I have a fabulous place to live, thanks to you."

"My pleasure. When my friends told me they were considering renting out their mother-in-law's cottage but were concerned about finding the right tenant, you immediately came to mind. That was an easy call, so think nothing of it. But how are *you* doing? How's the writing?"

"I'm pretty Unstuck, if that's what you mean. Mostly, that is."

"Oh? What's up?"

"It's just that . . . I keep thinking, how can all this be real? So much has changed so fast, and what if—"

"Aha! What if it's a mistake?"

"Yeah."

"Chloe, if this was a mistake, would your novel have been accepted for publication? Would you be called upon so often to contribute to *The New York Times* and *The Wall Street Journal*? Would you be invited onto cable shows to share your insights?"

"Well, when you put it like that . . ."

"*You* need to put it like that whenever these thoughts creep in. That's one of the reasons I'm calling. We haven't talked in weeks, and I wanted to check up on you. But I also wanted to update you. Remember that special surprise I mentioned?"

"Sure, but honestly, you've done so much for me already—"

"Bah! Listen, I can't share all the details yet, but I'd like you to keep the first week of August open for me. Can you do that?"

"Of course!"

"Good! I'll have more info soon, but in the meantime, keep up the good work."

"I will. Thanks so much, Sarah—for everything."

In the background, Chloe heard another phone ringing.

"That's my next conference call, so I have to run. Make sure to check your mailbox today!"

"What?"

But Sarah was gone.

"Mailbox? What's that about?" Chloe threw on a top over her camisole and headed to the main house to check the mail. As she made her way across the yard, Blanca appeared at the house's back door with a sizeable box.

"This came for you this morning, Miss Chloe," the maid said. "I was going to bring it to you after I cleaned up the kitchen."

"Thanks so much, Blanca," Chloe said, accepting the box and heading back to her bungalow with a spring in her step. What could it be?

She couldn't wait to grab the scissors from her desk and demolish the box. Once she unwrapped all the packing, she found a brand-new MacBook laptop! She immediately grabbed her phone and texted Sarah. *This is WAY too much! Oh my gosh! Thank you!*

Sarah immediately texted back. *Ur welcome. Now write!* ☺

Chloe sat and stared at her new computer, hardly believing her good fortune. Unpacking it and plugging it in, she got busy setting it up.

As she transferred files, she reflected once more on the rocket ship that had been the last six months. Since leaving *L.A. Local*, she'd written several opinion pieces for national publications, some of them expanding on her series about the local football team with the first female quarterback. One article dealt with the pros and cons of gender-specific sports, and how blurring the lines between the two by allowing both genders to compete together could be a good thing.

Another article focused on women's professional soccer and the issue of pay equality.

Men's soccer paid their players far more than women's, yet women's drew the larger crowds. The same with basketball. The larger the crowds, the more investment and sponsorships, creating a self-perpetuating cycle. So was the inequality justified? How could women's sports in general receive the attention and subsequent investment they deserved? Everyone had been rooting for the US Women's National Soccer Team just a few years ago, indicating a solution: it required a cultural shift that would see women's sports as entertaining as men's.

These kinds of questions fascinated Chloe, and she touched on as many as she could, bringing care and thought to the conversation. In the process, her articles garnered her more attention, and she was becoming an in-demand guest on a lot of cable shows.

She now had a consistent stream of invitations to write for major outlets, with more reaching out to her all the time. She spent a few hours each week fielding emails from newspapers and periodicals asking if she'd like to write on a variety of human-interest topics and current events— everything from business and politics to entertainment and even self-help.

She found that last one ironic. Sarah was the self-development expert, not her. So far, Chloe had yet to write anything about it. Despite her newfound success, she still felt as if she was faking it sometimes. Surely, it would soon be discovered that she wasn't as good as people believed. Then it would be back to the salt mines.

Imposter syndrome or not, Chloe remained committed to her principles. She'd decided long before that when writing about such issues, her approach would be thoughtful and measured, and if that decision hurt her prospects or diminished her readership, so be it. She wasn't interested in pushing hardline opinions filled with incendiary language. Her goal was to analyze all sides of an issue, empathize with those sides, and offer suggestions on how to promote reasonable discussion aimed at cooperative exploration, not uncompromising opinion.

She believed that the only way to contribute meaningfully to the marketplace of ideas was through open communication and a genuine desire to improve people's lives. And her approach resonated with audiences. Every piece she wrote received more web traffic and reader response than the last. With her latest article, she was shocked to find that she was entering territory where her writing itself was becoming news. Various articles and blurbs by other journalists and writers appeared in response to her work. She couldn't explain all the attention, but she liked to think it had to do with everyone's waning tolerance for clickbait titles and lack of real substance.

Somehow, Chloe found herself at the forefront of a new digital audience. Younger readers were coming full circle after a generation of shrinking attention spans and the need for instant gratification. People were starting to shun low-effort, superficial writing and actively seek out substantive content. Chloe had no idea why she was swiftly becoming one of the faces of the movement, but as readers in the thousands continued to flock to her on social media, she felt incredibly fortunate to be a part of it.

What still thrilled her was the amount of freedom she had to decide what she wanted to write, how to write it, and when. She was so used to writing what she was told. It was refreshing to write whatever she liked. She still had deadlines and parameters and preferences from her editors, but it was collaborative now. Best of all, she could keep her integrity intact. No more clickbait titles and writing pieces whose purpose was little more than selling ads. Now she could choose only the projects that resonated with her. Her biggest challenge was not to overpromise to her editors. She didn't want to bog herself down with so much work that the quality of her writing suffered. That was a refreshing challenge to have.

Chloe was finally getting Unstuck, living a fulfilling life, and writing work she wanted to write. She felt healthier and happier and had more energy than ever before. On top of that, she no longer suffered under the crushing weight of mountainous debt and the chronic stress it caused. It made her feel as if she were positively floating.

Sitting in front of her laptop, sipping her coffee, she realized she had zoned out again, lost in appreciation for her new life. Shaking off the daydreams, she focused on her current projects. She wanted to finish the outline for book two of her trilogy, and maybe putter with the premise and outline for another series she had in mind.

Before any of that, however, she had a few articles with fast-approaching deadlines. Having transferred her files and accounts to her new

MacBook, she opened her calendar and Word program. *The Wall Street Journal* wanted their piece on the mental health cost of social media versus its vital importance in the world of marketing. The *Los Angeles Times* wanted their next piece on the proposed late start times for California's schools. And she had a video call in a few days with an editor at *The New York Times*. They were interested in working with her on a national think piece.

She also had an interview scheduled at the end of the week with a popular news podcast called the Daily Dot. The show producers were fans of her writing and wanted to pick her brain on a few pieces of hers. She had to review their list of questions and do a little prep, and she also wanted to listen to a few of their most popular episodes to get a feel for their specific vibe.

All in all, a busy week ahead. She had a few other offers she was still contemplating, and a laundry list of errands and chores to tend to, including meeting with her new financial advisor. She found that last one funny. Now that she actually had some funds and an ever-growing income, she had to start thinking about health insurance, saving for retirement, and investing—all the financial stuff she'd always been too broke to consider. As a freelancer, she couldn't rely on the company to take care of those things for her in a benefits package. She had to create her own, which just added to the wild transformation her life had become.

She smiled again. If things kept going the way they were going, she'd be looking for a house or a condo within a year or so. But for now, she was just happy to finally be out of debt. Her credit score was skyrocketing, and credit card companies were tripping over themselves, increasing her card limits and offering new cards with better terms—a few of which looked pretty attractive. She'd have to talk it over with her accountant.

Through it all, she continued to "Review, rethink, rewrite." It had become her mantra, and she implemented the three R's several times a week, practicing the lessons she'd learned at the Unstuck conference, refining her approach, uncovering new wisdom and new insights about herself. She also had a new goal card, which she laminated not too long ago. Rewritten in a way that made it more powerful, she carried it in her phone case, taking it out from time to time to let the words wash over her: *I am so grateful my writing changes the world.*

She also finally got back into the habit of keeping a journal. It gave her a sense of structure for the day, writing on everything from work and the Unstuck program to her personal life and future goals. It was quickly becoming an integral part of her self-care, centering her and helping her sort out her thoughts and feelings. These ongoing practices were vital, allowing her to stay on top of everything, and she couldn't wait to hear the final six lessons.

Chiding herself, she switched her focus once again to the work in front of her. Checking her inbox, the first unread mail gave her pause.

Remember me?

The contact name was F. Capone. It rang a bell, but she couldn't place it. Spam, maybe? She clicked it, not recognizing the email address either. Scrolling to the bottom to find the sender, her eyebrows shot up. "Holy cow!" she said aloud. It was from Frank, her old boss at *L.A. Local*! Smiling, she read it through.

> *Hey Chloe,*
> *I'd say I hope you're doing well, but I've been keeping an eye on your career since you left the Local, and you're clearly doing more*

than OK. LOL. Congrats on all your success. Your latest articles are the best you've ever written. Can't wait to see what you do next.

I took a page out of your playbook and made some upgrades myself. I left the Local about a month ago. I accepted a position at SFGATE. I feel like a new person. More on all that later, if you want.

To be honest, I half-expect the reason I got this job in the first place was because I worked with you. That was a big talking point during the interviews. I hope it doesn't bother you, but I kind of promised I'd at least reach out to you to see if you'd like to collab on something.

They'd love to have you do a local piece on Bay Area culture or a human-interest story. There are lots of options, and of course you could bring your own ideas to the table. I'm sure you're incredibly busy, but maybe it's something you'd be interested in sometime?

On another note, I've done more than take a page from your playbook. I've stolen it. Right after you left, I signed up for online courses at Sarah's PG Institute. I've been slowly making my way through the six *lessons, and I can see why you adopted the program. It's gutsy. New territory for me. I don't do the transparency thing well. I'm having trouble with some of it. The online seminars and discussion boards are great, but I thought maybe talking with someone I know might be more helpful.*

If you'd like to talk shop, just catch up, or both, I can catch a quick flight down to L.A. on the Gate's dime, so just let me know. Working for a company that has an actual budget has its perks.

Miss you. Bet you never thought you'd hear that, huh?

Frank

Chloe leaned back and let out a long breath. *Frank?* The Frank who would scream at her from across the office? The Frank who hung up on her a hundred times? This was a side of him she'd never seen before—except maybe once, when they had toasted her departure from *L.A. Local*.

She smiled as she typed a quick reply. He was working at SFGATE now? She was so happy for him. They were one of San Francisco's biggest news websites. Owned by the same company as the *San Francisco Chronicle*, the Gate and the *Chronicle* had branched off into separate entities some years ago. Chloe couldn't believe it. Frank had been at the Local for ages. She thought he'd be there until he dropped. This was a ginormous career upgrade.

Shaking her head, she thought back on their contentious relationship. He'd always been rough around the edges, with the two of them butting heads more often than not. But deep down, he was a good man. That was half the reason she'd stuck around all those years. Typing away, she told him she'd be happy to hang out and catch up, and she'd love to do an article for the Gate. She suggested next week or the week after, at a particular diner near the Burbank airport.

Hitting *send*, she perused the rest of her inbox, finding a long-awaited message from Sarah. *Great day for email!* she thought, opening it.

> *Hello, Chloe!*
>
> *Chloe, Chloe, my friend Chloe! It was great chatting this morning. Sorry I had to jump off so fast.*
>
> *Of course, you know I devour everything you write, and your latest articles are won-*

derful. I put in a preorder for a copy of your first novel. Congratulations again! That's why I wanted to get you the laptop. I would hate for you to lose some of your prose with a computer crash.

All the pieces are finally in place, and I'm ready to share the big surprise. I'm inviting you and a small group of other remarkable professionals to a special work retreat at Meadowood Napa Valley. It's a five-star luxury resort in the heart of wine country. I've been a patron of the place for years. It's perfect for both business and pleasure!

The retreat is a week long, and it's scheduled for the first week of August. That should give everyone time to make room in their schedules, especially since August tends to be a slower month for most people. Travel, food, and accommodations are all taken care of, so just pack some clothes and prepare yourself for some well-earned pampering.

And I do mean pampering. This won't be all work and no play. Check it out online. www.relaischateaux.com/us/hotel/meadowood-napa-valley/. It's serious. We'll have a meeting each morning for a few hours, and the rest *of the day will be yours. I've even scheduled a private dinner for us at the French Laundry, just down the road. This area is wine and foodie heaven, so be prepared to indulge!*

It's important to me that everyone be able to unplug, leave their responsibilities behind, and focus on contemplating the new lessons in whatever way works best for them. Between the wineries in the area, spa, fitness studio, your luxury suite, and the resort's various activities, there are plenty of ways to relax and have fun while you let the lessons simmer on the back burner of your mind.

RSVP when you have a moment. I hope you can make it, and I can't wait to reconnect with you properly!

Much love,
Sarah

Chloe's cheeks were burning from all the smiling. She replied right away, letting Sarah know she would absolutely be there. After hitting *send*, she looked up Meadowood. She'd heard of it in passing, knowing it was the kind of place she could only ever dream of staying at, so she never bothered to check it out. Browsing the website, she couldn't help laughing aloud. It was easily the most luxurious place she'd ever seen. Everything was simple and elegant, nestled in a lush green setting in the middle of wine country, and the suites were as big as her cottage! Letting out a deep breath, she was glad her publisher had already given her an advance on the next two books. She was going to need some new clothes and a little spending money for the retreat.

CHAPTER TWO

FRANK

A few weeks later, Chloe took the 134 to Burbank, pulling into a Mexican restaurant that was a favorite of the locals. There wasn't much atmosphere amongst the simple wooden tables and chairs, but the place was always packed. The food was that good. She found Frank at a booth near the door, thumbing through the menu. She could barely believe her eyes. He looked thirty pounds lighter and ten years younger.

"Frank!" she said, throwing her messenger bag on the seat and hugging him as he got up to greet her. "You look amazing! I never knew you were so handsome. Oh my gosh, is that a tan?"

Frank gave her a sheepish smile as they slid into the booth. "Good to see you, Chloe. Yeah, the wife and I have been getting out a bit more."

"I should say so! How is Claire?"

"She's good, she's good."

Chloe knew her response was making him uncomfortable. She'd never seen him squirm like that. It was hilarious. "It's obvious that change suits you. I'm so proud of you."

His eyes met the table again before glancing up at her. "You're not looking too shabby yourself. This program of hers, huh?" He shook his head.

"Yeah, it has an effect, doesn't it?" Chloe agreed. A server approached, and Chloe held up her glass for water.

"What can I get youse?" the server said, snapping her chewing gum as she filled Chloe's glass.

"Could I get the chicken fajitas?" Chloe said.

"I'll just have a, uh, house salad," Frank said. "Italian on the side."

"Coming right up," the server said, jotting on a notepad as she moved off.

Chloe stared slack-jawed at him, continuing to play up her reaction. "Frank Esquire Capone, did you just order a salad? With lettuce and carrots?"

He smiled, waving her toward him. "Come on, get it out of your system. Any other jabs? You done? And my middle name isn't Esquire. Where did you even get that?"

Chloe laughed. "I'm sorry, it's just . . . Frank, everything about you feels like I'm talking with a new man. How much of this is Unstuck, and how much of it is Claire?"

"Definitely both," Frank said, chuckling. "Ever since I showed her the work I was doing on myself, she's been all about it. She dove in with both feet, and we've been working the lessons pretty much together. She's having an easier time of it than me, but we're both getting a lot out of it. I wish she'd lay off the diet and exercise a little, but she's taking this whole thing and running with it, insisting it's important we take the opportunity to work on all aspects of our lives." He shrugged. "I still sneak the occasional burger when she's not looking."

"But not today?" Chloe asked.

"Not today. Eating light helps with work. Keeps me sharp."

"Glad to hear it. Same with me. I'm headed to a resort in a few weeks, and I want to look and feel my best."

"A resort?" Frank said. "Nice. Time for a little rest and relaxation?"

"Kind of. Sarah invited a small group to a week-long retreat at Meadowood, in Napa. She's going to take us through the final six lessons of Unstuck."

Frank's eyes grew wide. "Meadowood? Wow! That place is as ritzy as they come. Like a grand a night, and that's *if* you can get in."

"Yeah, I took a look at their website. It's like for royalty. Pretty crazy."

"Well, don't send me any pictures of the place. I don't want Claire getting any ideas."

Chloe laughed. "No worries there. I'll just send them to her instead."

"Don't you dare," Frank smiled, wagging a finger. "She's heard about these next six lessons, and she's chomping at the bit to get into them. She doesn't need any more encouragement. Either way, she'll probably start them without me. A few things just aren't clicking for me yet."

"You mentioned that. I'm not sure what kind of help I can be, but we can certainly talk about it."

Frank shuffled in his seat. "Thanks. I don't know. I'm just not very good with this stuff."

"I get it," Chloe said. "And I'm sure it doesn't help that we're both so used to being colleagues.

It's hard to shift away from that formal, professional relationship. Though, given how much we argued, we were never really that formal." They both chuckled. "But I think that fact can serve us. Unstuck does make you take a pretty hard look at yourself." She ducked her head, raising his gaze to meet hers. "But, c'mon. We've known each other for a long time. We've put in some crazy hours, working side by side, keeping the Local afloat. We know each other well enough to stretch ourselves a bit. Would it make you feel any better if I said I promise not to write about you?"

Frank scoffed. "Only if you want to tank your career. I hear you, though. And I know. It's just weird. I'm not your boss anymore, and you're much more Unstuck than I am. You're like Sarah's star pupil, I bet. I'm not used to being the subordinate."

Chloe squinted at him, a playful smile on her lips. "Sucks, doesn't it?"

Frank waved her on again. "That's it, get your jabs in. Go ahead."

"Well, Frank, there's no more power dynamic between us. We're equals. We're just two people, each getting ourselves on the other side of being stuck. It's not a competition, which is a hard thing for people like us to accept. Journalism is tough. We're hardwired to be competitive. That can be a good thing, but it just doesn't apply here."

Frank twirled his glass of water. "Yeah, you're right. It's going to take some getting used to. Speaking of hardwiring, I think that's probably the elephant in the room." He shrugged. "I've just never looked at life the way I'm being asked to. My old man was a real John Wayne type, you know? Put the work in, provide for your family, be the rock everyone leans on. That's how I grew up.

"I had a good childhood, don't get me wrong. I loved my dad, but it was tough. He always told me, 'Frank, you've got broad shoulders for a reason.' He taught me that whatever life threw at you, you just carried it. And that included your emotions. They're not meant to be displayed or indulged, let alone analyzed. They're meant to be carried, along with everything else. He was like Atlas that way. The world on his shoulders."

He leaned forward, dropping his voice a little. "Right after you left the Local, I gotta tell you. It was tough. I didn't realize how much we depended on you."

Chloe smiled. It was good to hear that, even if it was in the past.

Frank continued. "I had an epiphany at the office that first Monday you were gone. I'm sitting there, files everywhere, emails piling up, phone ringing off the hook, a line of people at the door waiting to talk to me. All I could think about was the smile on your face when we raised our glasses the afternoon you left."

Frank pointed to Chloe's face. "See? There it is! You're still smiling!"

Chloe put her hand over her mouth. "Oh, I didn't realize. It's not that it's funny. I'm not sure where it's coming from."

"I am. It's one of the few truly happy faces I think I've ever seen. When you left my office, I realized I had for a fleeting moment looked into the face of a truly happy human. I spent that whole weekend thinking about it. I'd never seen you so happy. But it was more than happiness. It was . . . everything I was looking for. Relief, excitement, anticipation, like joy. You were beaming and at peace all at once. I knew there was more to it than handing in your resignation. Unstuck had done something to you—*for* you. You were different in ways I couldn't fathom."

He paused, gazing over her shoulder at nothing. "I remember thinking, *I want that*. And then I was hit with a tidal wave of frustration and anger and a sadness deeper than anything I'd felt in my life. In that moment, over twenty years of toil and effort caught up with me, hitting me all at once. I was pretty miserable. I'd spent my adult life with my eyes closed. Sitting at my desk, watching you walk out of my office with that smile, the phone ringing and the staff knocking on my door, I knew it was time. I had to go. All of a sudden, I realized what a prison I was in—a prison I had embraced for years. If you could find it, well, I had to find it too. For better or worse, I had to make some major changes."

He shook his head. "Anyway, something's been nagging me about that day, and I finally figured out what. Yeah, it was a life-changing moment, but there was also a lot of shame attached to it. It's like my shoulders finally gave out, and everything came crashing down. Part of me feels like it's the last thing I should be proud of. It feels like I let my dad down." He took a deep breath. "I don't know. He passed over ten years ago, and I'm still trying to live up to him. Anyway, that's kind of where my head is at lately."

Chloe was thrilled, and more than a little surprised. This was more than Frank had ever shared about his life. It must have been hard for him. "Whether analyzing your emotions is a good thing or a bad thing, you're pretty good at it, Frank. Since you know your Greek mythology, there's a fine line between Atlas and Sisyphus."

"Which one was Sisyphus?"

"He was condemned to an eternity of pushing a boulder up a hill, only for it to roll back down when he reached the top. I don't mean to disparage your father or say he was wrong in any way, but carrying the weight of your emotions on your shoulders may be the definition of hell. It's an exercise in futility. There are a lot of ways to deal with life, Frank. What's most important is that you find what works best for you. If that means Atlas has to shrug, then so be it. There's a great line in *Atlas Shrugged*. 'What greater wealth is there than to own your life and to spend it on growing?'"

"There is no greater wealth," Frank said, looking into Chloe's eyes, fighting back tears.

Chloe smiled. "I think the main thing is that your father sounded like a good man. I doubt he'd begrudge you finding a way forward that suited you. It's not like his lessons went unheeded. Look how far they've gotten you. You and Claire have been together since high school, you put two kids through college, you got the house, the white picket fence, the whole nine yards. You don't need to worry about making him proud. You already have."

"I hope so," Frank said, lacing his hands together and placing them atop his head as he leaned back. "Is this what talking to Sarah is like for you?"

Chloe laughed. "If it's helping you, then yeah. To that end, I'm all yours for any questions or issues. I can't guarantee I'll have the answers, but I'm happy to keep talking through any aspect of Unstuck you want. If I learn anything I think might be of help on this retreat, I'll be sure to pass it along to you. Any questions I can't answer, I'll take to Sarah herself. I can keep you anonymous, if you prefer. So don't worry. We'll get the answers you need and keep you on track, one way or another."

Frank nodded, looking down at his glass. "Thanks, Chloe."

"You have my info, so text or email whenever you want. Especially during the retreat."

"You sure?"

"Yeah, of course. I'll have direct access to Sarah, plus these other folks at Unstuck Two. Maybe they can help as well. I bet they're pretty advanced in getting Unstuck, probably further along than I am. We're spending the mornings on the lessons and discussion. The rest of the time is ours to relax and reflect. I'll have plenty of time. If we want to set up a call, we can do that too."

"How did I ever let you walk out of my office that day?" Frank asked.

"You didn't let me walk out. I chose to leave. Just like you did. These are decisions each of us needs to make on our own."

"You're right, of course," Frank said. "I won't forget that."

The server arrived with their food. "Can I get youse anything else?"

"You good?" Frank asked Chloe.

"All set," Chloe replied.

"Thanks," Frank told the server.

"All right, enjoy," she said, snapping her gum with a smile.

Frank let out a deep sigh as he dripped Italian dressing over his salad. "Well, the Gate's paying for this, so I suppose we ought to talk some shop, if you're willing."

"Absolutely," Chloe said around a mouthful of fajita. "But first, Frank. The Gate? Seriously, congrats on that! Really proud of you."

"Yeah, thanks. I'm as surprised as anyone. I'll be fifty-one this year. I didn't think anyone would take me on, let alone an outfit like the Gate."

"Your level of experience is hard to come by," Chloe said. "You bring a lot of grit. That counts for a lot. They put you in charge of a department?"

"Yeah, assistant editor of sports. It's a test run. Gives me time to get acclimated and sets me up to take over the department. My boss is leaving, heading out for New York in a few weeks."

"Great timing. I gotta say, I thought for sure you'd stay at the Local forever."

Frank snorted. "You and me both. I figured they'd find me keeled over my desk someday. Anyway, things have been going great at the Gate, so Claire and I are in the process of selling the house in Pasadena. We're still shopping around for something near the Bay Area. Housing prices are high right now, but so's my new salary. We should be able to find a decent apartment. I'm just hoping the commute won't be too long."

"That's so great, Frank. I bet Claire's ecstatic."

"Oh, yeah. Partly because of the move and new job, but mostly because of my working with Unstuck. Like you said, she says I'm like a new man."

"She's getting to know the guy under the John Wayne façade."

Frank laughed. "Yeah, and so far, she likes what she sees."

"And you?"

"Yeah, me too." He took a bite of salad. "All right, enough of that stuff. Let's get down to business."

Chloe snorted, almost choking on her food. "You got it, boss. What's the job?"

"Everything's fair game. This is all open to discussion, but ideally, our features editor was thinking of something that mixes business, culture, and current events. Something that appeals to young professionals, but also has some emotional depth, all through the lens of today's social and political climate. Something savvy, thoughtful, and helpful. The higher-ups were thinking something along the lines of the nature of success. And since you've exploded on the scene as the country's hottest new journalist, they thought it'd be perfect for you. What do you think?"

Chloe smiled. "I don't know about that last bit, but yeah, that sounds intriguing."

"Yeah?" Frank said. "Good. We can do a one-off, but they're more interested in making this a series. Say, three to six installments over the next six months to a year. You can delve into what younger generations are facing as they claw their way to the top, how it differs from previous generations, and maybe give some opinions on what things might look like in the future. Do some digging on a few major industries, like tech and tourism, and see where it takes you. What do you think?"

"I love it," Chloe said. "I've been keeping a journal, and a lot of what's on my mind has to do with this kind of thing. To go from covering high school sports at the Local, to writing at the national level, to going on a multicity book tour all within a year has really got my head reeling. By exploring other industries, trends, and experiences, it would be a great way for me to really focus my thoughts and help me absorb everything that's happening. I'm definitely down for a series."

"Awesome. I'll let the brass know. Thing is, you'll be working with the features editor. I'm just an intermediary here. I think trying to get you to write for us is just part of the dues I have to pay for the job. So, going forward, I'll pretty much be out of the picture."

"Would it help your position if you continued working with me?" Chloe asked.

Frank paused. "I don't really know. It definitely wouldn't hurt."

"OK, how about this? I work with you on this project. You're my point of contact. You take it to the features editor and anyone else involved, and they give you their feedback, which you then bring to me. I want them to see that you are the guy."

Frank smiled. "Well, Miss Daniels, if you're making that an official contingency of the project, then I'm sure the brass will have no choice but to accept."

"It makes sense, doesn't it?" Chloe said with a laugh. "We fought a lot, but we worked really well together. It'll be smoother and more efficient for everyone involved. They'll tell you what they need, then you'll remove the sugarcoating and give it to me straight. If all this happens to elevate your standing at the Gate in the process, then win-win."

Frank was beaming from ear to ear. "I still get to yell at you, right?"

Chloe raised her water, and they clinked their glasses together. "If you can hear yourself over my own yelling, more power to you."

CHAPTER THREE

MEADOWOOD

Chloe spent the next two months wrapping up loose ends and juggling her August schedule. After a bit of shopping and some last-minute rewrites for her latest work, she was all set for the retreat. Even with all her recent success, she still wasn't comfortable spending a lot on herself. The what-ifs were always at the back of her mind. What if I don't get work and need to live off my savings? What if I have an emergency and don't have any company paid leave to rely on? What if . . . ?

Meanwhile, Sarah wasn't wasting any time with the surprises. On Sunday, instead of receiving plane tickets in her inbox, Chloe received directions to a private jet that would be waiting for her at Van Nuys Airport in the afternoon. "A private jet? First time for everything," she whispered to herself. She couldn't help feeling she was more than important. She felt valuable.

An Uber ride later, Chloe stood beside a small hangar with a sleek white jet in front of it. Two uniformed women exited the aircraft, coming down its small set of steps as she grabbed her luggage from the trunk. Meeting her halfway, one took her bags while the other held out her hand.

"Good afternoon, Miss Daniels. I'm Jane, your captain, and this is Charlie, my copilot. We'll be taking you to Meadowood today."

"Hi, thank you," Chloe said. "This is pretty amazing."

"First time flying private?" Jane asked.

"Yeah, can you tell?" Chloe laughed.

"Most people try to play it cool, but first-timers are always excited," Jane said. "I don't blame you. This is the Gulfstream 650, and it's an absolute dream to fly. It also happens to be Miss Garner's personal aircraft."

"Really?" Chloe said as they approached the steps leading inside.

"Sure is. She instructed us to coordinate with third-party charters to ensure the rest of your group arrived in a timely fashion, but she wanted to make sure that you got the star treatment. This sweetheart is designed for international travel. The trip to Meadowood is too short to show you what she's really capable of. Regardless, it's a beautiful day for flying, and you're going to have a wonderful trip."

Once inside, Chloe marveled at the interior. Bathed in white with rich, dark hardwood accents, it looked like a miniature mansion. A long, white leather sofa lined the right side, opposite a console with a wide-screen TV, both separated by a wide center aisle. Beyond that sat two rows of four seats, each as big as a recliner, and beyond those sat four more seats around a luxurious hardwood table. Two strips of inlaid LED lights ran the length of the ceiling, adding to the sunshine from the jet's many circular windows. She'd never seen anything like it.

"Please choose a seat you can buckle into for takeoff and landing," Charlie said. "Jane is going to start the pre-flight checklist while I get you settled. Now, we have a lovely California chardonnay on ice for you. Or I can make you a fresh espresso, if you prefer?"

"Oh, wow," Chloe said. "Um, the chardonnay would be great, thank you."

"Excellent choice," Charlie said. "I'm going to stow your luggage in the back, and I'll return in a moment with your wine."

Charlie moved down the aisle and through a doorway just beyond the table and chairs at the far end. Chloe chose the first seat past the sofa. Taking her laptop and phone from her messenger bag and setting them in the seat next to her, she also grabbed her journal, thinking she might write a new entry along the way.

"Here you are," Charlie said, handing her a glass of wine.

"Thank you," Chloe said. "How long to Napa?"

"Just about ninety minutes, once we're in the air. Is there anything else I can get you?"

"No, I'm all set, thanks."

"My pleasure," Charlie said. "We'll be taxiing onto the runway shortly, and we should be in the air in about fifteen minutes. We'll reach cruising altitude fairly quickly, at which point you'll be able to relocate to the sofa or wherever you like. We'll let you know over the intercom. If at any point you need anything, just press one of the call buttons located throughout the cabin."

"Wonderful, thanks so much."

"Enjoy the flight, Miss Daniels."

Moving up the aisle, Charlie raised the steps and secured the door before joining Jane in the cockpit. As she took a sip of the chilled wine, Chloe realized she was smiling. She couldn't keep her eyes off the cabin. She felt as if she were the first passenger on the jet's maiden voyage, it was so sparkling and pristine. Looking around as the thrum of the engines grew, she sipped again. "I could get used to this."

*   *   *

About an hour and a half later, a limousine met Chloe at the Sonoma County airport, whisking her away to Meadowood. Approaching the tree-lined drive to Meadowood's guardhouse, the chauffeur waved at the guard and proceeded through to the main building. She had heard of the destination for years. She never imagined she would be a guest.

"Thank you," she said to the chauffeur as she stepped from the limo. She took a moment to take it all in as he retrieved her luggage.

The resort looked like a graceful mansion from the front—unlike any hotel she'd ever stayed at. Green pathways led off to the side of the main building. Across the drive was the golf course, and she could hear tennis balls being hit in the distance nearby. Otherwise, it was serene, like something out of a postcard.

Her chauffeur carried her suitcase into what Chloe presumed was the lobby. It was as graceful, understated, and elegant as what she'd seen of the outside. Neutral tones and natural materials done with the utmost attention to detail all created a relaxed atmosphere. A gentleman at the front desk looked up and smiled.

"Miss Daniels?"

Chloe jumped. How did he . . . ? Then she smiled. Of course a place like this would know which guests to expect and when. "Yes, that's me."

"Welcome to Meadowood." He pulled out a key card and map of the resort. "You're staying in the Oakview Room, one of my favorites. It has a bright, airy feeling. Ms. Sarah thought would inspire your writing."

Chloe's cheeks were starting to hurt from all the smiling.

"Shall I take you to your room directly, or would you like to explore a little? I understand your party is meeting at the Terrace Café in thirty minutes."

"I think I'd like to freshen up first," Chloe said.

Following the attendant through the building and out the west exit, they walked down winding paths lined with lush gardens and luscious flowers with intoxicating fragrances. Their path wound around to showcase the bungalows and rolling hills of vineyards encircling the resort. It was as if the resort had been designed to fit with its surroundings.

He set her luggage inside the door, and she tipped him on his way out. She was thankful she had some cash on her. She'd have to hit an ATM somewhere and remember to keep some twenties on her for the rest of her stay.

Closing the door, she did everything she could to keep from squealing like a kid in a candy store. She did a dance instead. "What am I doing here?" she whispered as she turned in circles, kicking off her shoes. "When does the clock strike midnight and I have to go home?"

The jet was impressive. This place was outrageous. She'd done some more digging on her way here. Meadowood wasn't just some fancy resort. It was considered one of the top destination properties in the world. It was a palace. After all, it was a Relais & Chateaux hotel, one of the most exclusive hotel groups in the world. No, it was too big to be a palace—wrong vibe. It was like a palace estate. Was that a thing? She wasn't sure.

She walked toward the bed, closed her eyes, and did a swan dive face-first onto its luxurious pillows. Taking a few deep breaths into the organic linen duvet cover, the smell of fresh lilac calmed her racing heart.

Since the moment the limo had pulled onto the property, she had struggled to keep her composure. Just now, on her way inside the bungalow, she'd spied a baby grand piano next to a fireplace in an adjoining room. She couldn't believe this was happening. Less than six months ago, she'd had security bars on her apartment windows. Now they held a premium view of some of the world's most renowned vineyards.

She took a quick look around the room. The bathroom was to die for. A soaking tub rimmed in gray and white marble, a luxurious terry robe—with her name embroidered on it!—and enough Molton Brown products to keep her supplied for a month, not a week. Giving herself a once-over in the large mirror over the double sink, she wondered how long she'd had that silly grin on her face.

She used the mirror to straighten her outfit and freshen up. "Get hold of yourself. You said you could get used to this. Well, now's your chance." She leaned forward as she ran a hand through her hair and brushed the wrinkles from her blouse. She paused, lifting her chin and looking herself in the eyes. "Just remember. Someone believes you belong here. Let's find out why."

Chloe decided to wait on exploring the rest of her suite, afraid she'd spend the whole afternoon lost in its beauty, not to mention the amazing views out each window. Grabbing her things, she took off for the Terrace Café. She walked to the main building and asked the front desk for directions.

Out the south exit and down a broad, beautiful green with a large swimming pool on one side, she found several low outbuildings. The terrace near the so-called cabana pool led to the Terrace Café, a comfortable outdoor area that had the informal atmosphere of someone's luxury patio. The marble-topped bar stood at the back, where a number of black-clad waiters and bartenders attended the café's guests. She walked in and saw Sarah in a festive, floral sarong dress, ordering a bottle of wine from the bartender.

As Chloe approached, Sarah glanced in her direction and did a double take, a smile bursting onto her face. "Chloe, you made it!"

"In style, thanks to you!" Chloe laughed as the two embraced. "It's been months. Way too long away from the woman who changed my life," she whispered in Sarah's ear. "That jet of yours was incredible. Then the limo, and Meadowood itself is out of this world! I haven't even explored the suite yet. I'm doing my best not to walk around with my mouth hanging open."

"I'm so glad you enjoyed the trip," Sarah said, holding her at arm's length. "You're looking radiant."

"Thanks, you too. I love your dress. I'll need to do some shopping, upgrade my wardrobe for the week."

"Oh, Meadowood has some amazing boutique shops; you're going to love them. And there are even more in town. Let's go tomorrow, after the morning meeting."

"Awesome, can't wait!" Chloe said.

"I'm sorry we haven't talked more over the past few months. Things have been crazy. I've had this retreat in the works, so I knew we'd be catching up soon."

"It's no problem at all. Things have been pretty crazy for me too. More work than I can shake a stick at, and the publisher wants a trilogy."

"That's wonderful, congratulations!" Sarah said. "Are they talking book tour? Signings and interviews and all?"

"They mentioned it. I'm not sure how extensive it'll be yet, but it's pretty exciting."

"Just be sure to pace yourself. They're going to push your schedule to the limit. Don't be afraid to slow them down. Hopefully, they'll set you up with experienced book escorts."

"Good to know," Chloe said. "I bet your book tour for Unstuck was exhausting."

"Definitely. Ten cities in two weeks. We were all over the place. It was great fun, just a bit of a blur."

"Great advice, thanks," Chloe said, opening her purse. "I have a surprise for you, by the way." She pulled out a copy of her new book. "This is a reader's copy, so it's going to see some changes, but I thought you might like to look it over sometime."

Sarah gasped, taking the book gently, as if it were a priceless jewel. "*Sunset at Whisper Creek*," she murmured, stroking the cover. "Chloe, this is perfect. My favorite pastime on vacation is hanging out by the pool and reading. I can't wait; thank you so much!"

The bartender approached, holding out a bottle of wine for Sarah to inspect. Perusing the label, she nodded. "Yes, that's perfect, Sam. Two bottles should do it."

"You got it," Sam replied. "Your server will be out shortly."

"Thanks," Sarah said, turning back to Chloe. "Everybody's over there, at the big corner table on the patio. I thought we'd have a little meet and greet, just hang out and talk, then have menus passed around for something to eat. How's that sound?"

Chloe took an excited breath. "Sounds good to me!"

"Great, follow me," Sarah said, heading toward the back of the building. She put her arm around Chloe as they walked and gave her a squeeze. "Remember, don't be nervous. You belong here."

Chloe laughed. "I'll try."

*   *   *

The corner table Sarah had booked was semisecluded, under the canopy of an ancient oak tree.

As the breeze stirred the leaves, the quiet rustle helped Chloe unwind. No traffic, no phones, no computers. Just the beauty of this place and the company of these amazing people.

"Good news, all!" Sarah exclaimed. "Chloe has arrived!"

A cheer went up from about a dozen people gathered around a few tables.

Sarah turned to Chloe as they approached. "I've been talking you up a bit. They're excited to meet the world's next big fiction author."

Chloe waved her hand, embarrassed. She could feel the heat rise in her cheeks.

"As I've mentioned," Sarah continued to the group, "Chloe conducted a very popular interview with me at a small news outlet not too long ago, just as she began exploding onto the scene as a journalist of rare talent and voice. You may have read some of her stuff in the *L.A. Times*, *The Wall Street Journal*, and *The New York Times*, among others. What's more, she's landed a book deal, and her first novel is set to debut soon. Rumor has it, it's a shoo-in for the New York Times Bestseller List."

Small cheers and applause went around the room. "Great work, Chloe!" someone said above the response.

"Chloe has shown a remarkable understanding of what it takes to get Unstuck," Sarah continued, "developing her thinking to perfection. She was my first and easiest choice for this retreat, and I think you'll all be very happy that she's part of our group."

Another cheer went up, with shouts of "Welcome!" and "Yay, Chloe!" sprinkling through the applause.

"Chloe, this is the group!" Sarah said. "My goal was to assemble the most promising people in the world—those who have become a remarkable presence in their chosen field. Men and women providing innovative new ways of going about business and life itself." She spread her arms wide. "This group of humanity is our future. Each of you is going to make a difference, mark my words. I know that partly because of your goal cards. Every one of you has the same goal, worded in your own way."

Her eyes settled on Chloe. "You want to change the world. And I am going to see that you have everything you need to do it."

CHAPTER FOUR
THE BARRIER

Waking up in a bed bigger and softer than any she'd ever slept in, Chloe beat her alarm clock by over an hour, excited for her first day of the retreat. The evening at the Terrace Café had gone so well, she was surprised she'd even slept at all. All nine of the other members were fascinating in their own ways, from titans of industry to famous artists and musicians. A few of them were on the verge of becoming known the world over—like Chloe herself.

Fiddling with the espresso machine at the small kitchen area next to the dining table, she chuckled to herself. She wasn't sure why Sarah was so adamant about her trajectory. Chloe didn't feel intimidated by it, or by the other members. A few of them were household names, like Lisa Beaumont, the founder of Gaia Electric, the world's leading electric vehicle manufacturer.

And every Gen Z knew the name Ricardo Costa. Hailing from Brazil, he was founder and CEO of Ding!, the fastest-growing social media platform in the world. Many of these people were bona fide billionaires. It didn't bother Chloe. They all seemed friendly and down-to-earth. Maybe she was just finally growing comfortable and confident in her own skin. Their success didn't diminish her own, or who she was as a person.

Having successfully navigated the espresso machine, she grabbed her laptop and headed out to the private deck. Looking over the lush greenery, toward the rolling hills of vineyards in the distance through a canopy of mature trees in the foreground, she sipped the strong, rich brew over her daily email check. Frank had reached out again, talking a bit about his questions with his Unstuck journey. He was having trouble with the behavior aspect of paradigm shifts.

She read over the goal card he shared with her. She whistled softly. Wow, Frank wanted to be an author! Chloe smiled, glad he trusted her with that kind of transparency. It was clear he was working seriously on getting Unstuck, sharing such intimate information. His problem was going to be procrastination, something she'd wrestled with before. She set up a video call with him for later that afternoon.

After writing a bit in her journal, she took her time getting ready, exploring her suite as she went. The luxury of the place still gave her pause. The bright-white, open floor plan flowed from one room to the next seamlessly, with hardwood flooring, tasteful modern furniture, and gorgeous wall hangings throughout. She promised herself she'd try out the fireplace in the sitting room some quiet evening. A large dressing room led to a bathroom bigger than her bedroom at home, featuring a soaking tub, shower room, and vanity with two sinks. Clean lighting throughout highlighted the impressive tiling and chrome bath fixtures. She couldn't believe this would be her home for the next week.

Trying not to dawdle, she sat in the soaking tub for a few minutes, eager to try some of the luscious spa products left as complimentary gifts for the guests. The lavender and eucalyptus gel won this time. It was relaxing and invigorating all at once—just what she needed for this first day of the retreat. She took a shower, picked out a breezy, casual outfit, grabbed her messenger bag, and made her way to a place called the Study.

Sarah had told them they could find it down the hall from the ballroom, all part of a wing of the main building dedicated to events and gatherings. Arriving at nine o'clock, Chloe again had to pause. The room was sheer luxury. It was bright and airy, with exposed beams at the ceiling, a river rock fireplace, and upholstered chairs arranged around the room. At one side was a long oak table with captain's chairs arranged on each side.

More seating surrounded the fireplace, beyond which sat a lovely garden terrace with tables and chairs. The whole room felt open to light and air, and had a lovely indoor-outdoor flow, just like the rest of the resort. Chloe took a deep breath and relaxed.

Most of the group had already arrived, and they were spaced throughout the room in small groups, chatting over coffee. Chloe made her way to a small refreshments table and poured herself a cup. No sooner had she finished than Sarah entered with her assistant Joyce, both carrying a medium-sized cardboard box.

"Good morning, everyone!" Sarah said as the two placed the boxes on an end table near the fireplace. "I trust you all found your suites up to snuff?"

"Absolutely!" Min cried. The group laughed, including Chloe. She liked Min. The young Asian woman had a presence three times her diminutive size, exuding an undeniable confidence. As an up-and-coming leader in the STEM field, her confidence made her all the more admirable.

"Glad to hear it," Sarah replied. "If you'll all gather round, Joyce and I have a little swag for you." Opening the boxes, the two began passing out luxurious leather messenger bags. Joyce caught Chloe's eye and winked, mouthing a quiet *hi* as Sarah continued. "Inside these lovely Saffiano leather workbags, provided by our friends at Prada, you'll find some familiar supplies that will help you through the week, along with a few surprises—binders containing lessons seven through twelve, beautiful leather-bound journals for documenting your journey, various pens, pencils, highlighters, and other office supplies, and best of all, a personalized Montblanc fountain pen engraved with your name."

A murmur of awe and appreciation went up as the group of ten collected their bags.

"For this first meeting," Sarah continued, "I thought we'd sit at the big table. As the week progresses, we can lounge around wherever we like, making the meetings as informal and comfortable as possible. That's why I chose the Study. It's big enough that we can all spread out, yet small enough that we can talk as a group no matter where we're sitting."

A few minutes later, everyone was settled at the big table. Sarah began.

"Well, here we all are. At last! I want to thank you for making the time in your busy schedules. You were all introduced to the first phase of Unstuck through a conference either here in the US or abroad. In every case, you were joined by hundreds to thousands of others. My desire with these next lessons is to provide you with a more intimate experience. There can be more of a dialogue between us. Instead of me talking at you, we can have a conversation.

"I split most of my time between conferences and retreats, although the retreats are rarely this fancy. I've been holding intimate gatherings like this one for years at other resorts throughout the country, and at a number of others in London, Paris, and a few other places abroad.

"What separates this retreat from all others is that you were specifically invited, and at no cost to you. Every other retreat we've ever held, the experience has been first come, first served, with a pretty significant price tag attached.

"A year ago, I started to see some remarkable people coming through our doors, and it occurred to me that I should hold a special retreat for those I believe stand out from the crowd, as talented, accomplished, and deserving individuals. This week is for those who are going to do more than innovate in their field. Those who have done more than simply become Unstuck to produce remarkable results.

"One of my talents is finding others with talent. Those people, no matter how successful they've already become, possess unique qualities, and if given the chance to elevate, they can make a lasting impact on the world.

"This week is for you. Each of you possesses those qualities, and I want to do everything in my power to unleash them."

Sarah looked around the room. "This week is costing me how much, Joyce?"

"One-point-two million," Joyce replied.

The room gasped.

"One-point-two million, people." She leaned toward the group and locked her eyes on each member. "And I want my money's worth. Deal?"

A small cheer and round of applause went up.

"Now," Sarah continued, "you all got to know a little about each other last night, so I'll forego the stuffy, awkward introductions. Over the course of the retreat, there will be plenty of time to become friends. Shall we jump right in?"

Another murmur of excitement flowed from the gathering.

"Wonderful," Sarah said. "Here we go, people. The secret lessons on getting Unstuck. Let's get number seven taken care of. It's a beautiful day, and I want to go swimming."

A wave of chuckles went over the group as they cracked the covers of their binders. Chloe hid a deep breath as she glanced around at the others. This was going to be awesome.

Sarah took her open binder and got up from the table, walking a few feet away. "As you know from the conferences, I think better when I wander a little bit. Feel free to do the same. I totally get it. For some of us, learning and thinking is a full-body experience.

"These morning meetings are all about comfort. But looking at the seventh principle, it's not very comfortable at all. I call it the Terror Barrier. Let's get into what it is, how it holds us back, and what we are going to do about it.

"At the top of your journal, you'll find another quote from yours truly: 'Fear and growth go hand in hand. When you courageously face the thing you fear, you produce the growth you have been seeking.'

"The Terror Barrier is strategically placed. While some have bumped headfirst into their terror barrier before this point in the program, it's only now many are ready to understand its nature and do something about it."

Chloe looked around and smiled. Nobody was writing. Pens were suspended in the air above their journals. They were drinking in every word Sarah spoke.

Sarah winked at her before continuing. "What is the Terror Barrier? In short, it's a construct of our paradigm. As we know, conscious thought leads to subconscious feelings, and these emotions are internalized to form our habits, our paradigm. The thing about paradigms is that we grow *very* comfortable with them. All paradigms hold us back, because they prevent us from thinking new thoughts.

"When we start to make progress toward our goals, when we make serious efforts to move out of our comfort zone and make significant changes to our lives, we run up against the Terror Barrier, courtesy of our paradigm. It's designed to keep us from making any major changes to our behavior. It says, 'Whoa, wait a minute, here. There's no telling where THIS will lead. The likelihood of it leading to those lofty goals of yours is nada. Best to stay here, where it's safe. Stop rocking the boat! You're upsetting the natural order of things.'"

Joyce brought Sarah a cup of coffee from the refreshments table. "Thanks," Sarah continued. "Trying to make major changes in order to achieve major goals, with no understanding of how to go about it properly, inevitably leads to your personal Terror Barrier. Stuck again.

"Popular theories focus on changing the external before changing the internal. Of course, this is because they produce a little buzz and some quick gratification, and people-helpers can make a lot of money off the illusion of change.

"But as we know, change starts within us, not with the world around us. Our behaviors are the temperature, our paradigm is the thermostat, and the world is the thermometer. You can't change the temperature by messing with the thermometer. You have to adjust the thermostat. You have to change your paradigm."

Sidney squinted at her husband, Tom. "Reminds me of that problem certain people have about getting out of their own way."

The group chuckled as Sarah nodded. "That's exactly right!"

Tom bumped Sidney's shoulder with his own as the two smiled at each other. The couple had met in college, working on degrees in software engineering. After spending years developing some important logistics software, they sold their company to pursue their true passions of art and music.

Chloe was fascinated to find artists in the room. She figured it would just be business types. She was glad to know that everyone could benefit from what Sarah and Unstuck had to offer. She wondered how the couple had made a name for themselves in the creative space.

"We've been conditioned to believe that it's better to be safe than sorry," Sarah said. "It's a wrong idea. I like to repeat important things, remember?" She looked around the room and smiled. "It's wrong. Safe misery is better than taking risks in the pursuit of your goals? I don't think so."

She took another sip of coffee. "As we look over the next few pages, the lesson uses our Stickperson from lesson four to describe the four steps in the psychological process of experiencing growth dealing with the Terror Barrier. They are bondage, reason, conflict, and freedom.

"Bondage is the trap you were in before you met me. You were getting unsatisfactory results because of your poor paradigm.

"Reason illustrates that although we're consciously creating the *idea* of the results we want, we don't act on it because we haven't internalized the idea and emotionally connected with it. You'll remember that vibration we talked about.

"Conflict comes into play when we finally make that emotional connection. The connection conflicts with our conditioning, completely messing with us. We become anxious and distressed as our brain and body go haywire with this conflict. Your emotional grasp of your idea is pulling you forward, while the conditioning of your old paradigm is pulling you backward. The voice is loud in your head, begging you to stay here, where it's safe.

"This part of your thinking is crucial. This is where you need tools and practices that encourage you. By summoning your courage and being diligent in your belief in yourself, you absolutely can break through that Terror Barrier and reach your desired outcome and last step—freedom.

"The most limiting aspect of the paradigm shift, for anyone, will always be ignorance. The Terror Barrier tells you that you don't know how to make your goals a reality, and that your resources and skills are inadequate. It insists that it's all too much, and the only safe course of action is to abandon these crazy dreams altogether. The Terror Barrier's entire argument is based on ignorance.

"Is that a surprise? Ignorance has always been and always will be a curable state to those courageous enough to keep moving forward—through knowledge, study, understanding, faith, and well-being.

"Just like with the conferences, there are exercises in the journal, both for the individual and the team, for those of you implementing the program with your teams. As always, there are the Three R's, which are . . . ?"

"Review, rethink, rewrite!" the group said in unison.

"Excellent job—you remembered!" Sarah said. "Let me stress, the Terror Barrier is a crucial idea in our time together. Plan to revisit it often. You'll be surprised at how profound it truly is. When the time comes for exercises, feel free to group up or work alone, whatever you like.

"Remember, after we review the exercises, the day is yours. Stay here and study, go to the cabana pool or the fitness pool, go shopping, hit the spa, whatever. Ponder the day's lesson throughout your stay, and consider meeting up with one another for a walk or a drink or a meal, to compare notes, help each other, and maybe even make a new friend. Any questions?"

Lisa, the electric vehicle manufacturer, raised a hand. "Are we meeting in the Study every morning? I love this room."

The group turned to Sarah, murmuring their agreement.

Sarah spread her arms wide. "You bet. I booked it for the entire week."

CHAPTER FIVE

Frank and Sarah

The group had a profitable time working on the exercises, talking until the question of lunch began to crop up. Where had the morning gone? Chloe had forgotten that she'd scheduled a video call with Frank at one, so she said quick good-byes and headed back to her bungalow, promising Sarah that she'd join her later at the resort's sundries shop.

Back at her suite, she grabbed a mineral water from the fridge and ordered a Caesar salad from room service. Settling on the terrace, she made some notes on her laptop in preparation for her call with Frank.

She shook her head as she glanced at her watch. She was going to have to get used to time passing so quickly here. This entire week would be over before she knew it. No sooner had she opened the video meeting than an alert popped up, showing that Frank was ready to join.

"Hi, Frank! How's it going?"

"Hey, Chloe. Never mind me. How's the retreat so far?"

"It's unreal, to be honest," Chloe laughed, turning herself and her laptop around so Frank could see her surroundings. "Check this place out."

"Oh, wow," Frank breathed. "Definitely don't tell Claire about this place."

"What?" a voice chimed in next to Frank. Claire appeared at his shoulder, bending low to fit herself in the camera frame. "Hi, Chloe! Frank says you're hitting the big time, and it looks like he's right!" She turned to Frank. "What am I not supposed to see, Franklin?"

Chloe laughed. "Hi, Claire. It's been a long time. I'd say things are going pretty well for all of us, these days."

"You got that right," Claire replied. "All thanks to you. Thank you for knocking this lug out of his rut. He may not say so, but take it from me. He's never been happier."

"I'm so glad," Chloe said. "You guys deserve it."

"Thank you, dear," Claire said. "Now help me convince him that we deserve a weekend at that resort of yours."

Frank groaned. "Do you have any idea how much—"

"Oh, bah," Claire said. "It'd do you good."

"I'm sure," Frank retorted. "It's got nothing to do with their fancy spas or shops or the wineries or anything, right?"

"We'll see about all that when the time comes," Claire stated.

Frank rolled his eyes with a sigh as Chloe clapped a hand over her mouth to keep from laughing.

"Good to see you, sweetie!" Claire said, waving. "Best of luck with the book!"

"Thanks, Claire, good to see you too!"

Just as suddenly as she'd appeared, Claire was gone, leaving Frank to stare daggers at her back. He cleared his throat with a huff. "Anyway, how's the week going? How's the group?"

"The first day was a doozy, I'll tell you. Fascinating stuff, and it hit at just the right moment. I think you're going to love this one, especially given what you said in your email about working through the Unstuck journal. Thanks for sharing your goal card, by the way. It's so exciting you want to publish. Any projects in the works?"

Frank nodded, flipping through a much-used legal pad, its pages covered in notes and scribbles. "Yeah, I'd like to write something about my old man and his time in the war. Not sure if it'll be a biography or if I'll just fictionalize it. Outside of that, I've got some ideas for the thriller genre. You know, the crack journalist who gets in over his head and breaks a huge story wide open."

"It's all about the story, Frank. Think through who your reader will be. Write what you know, so a protagonist who's a reporter makes perfect sense. You'll bring realism to a character like that. The story itself too."

Frank shrugged. "I don't know. I haven't written a full piece since my beat days over ten years ago. Since becoming an editor, I do more delegating than actual writing. I've spent the past decade telling people what to write, not doing any of my own. You know the drill."

"Every story you tweaked before going to press, you improved. You punched up countless stories at the Local, including mine, including the football team story. You're a writer, Frank. You have to find your story. When you find it, the story tells itself."

"Yeah, maybe." Frank flipped a few more pages of his legal pad, finally settling on the one he was looking for. "The problem is, I sit down to write, and I can't. It's not writer's block or anything. I just kind of freeze up. The idea seems so big, and I don't know how to start. It's like I psych myself out, convincing myself I'm better off waiting for a more opportune time, or maybe I'm better off just shelving the entire idea. Getting published is no easy feat, even for established journalists with big-shot connections like Chloe Daniels."

Chloe laughed. "It's not easy, I'll agree with you there. You think it has to do with changing your paradigm? You're probably still in that process, I imagine."

"Yeah, definitely. Lesson three talks about finding the cause of your negative behavior in order to change it. Well, I want to stop hand-wringing and actually tackle one of these book ideas." He shook his head. "But . . . I don't know."

"Hm," Chloe said, thinking back on her take-aways from Lesson Three. "I think I had this specific issue when I was at your stage. Not about writing per se, but about changing my paradigm. I was getting good at picturing what I wanted. You know, forming the idea of the results I wanted and internalizing it. I became emotionally attached to it, and it connected and fueled my behavior."

"Yeah, I've been practicing that, and as far as I can tell, I've got it down. Creating the ideal fantasy, envisioning myself having achieved my results. I see myself surrounded by stacks of my books, signing them for a line of people leading around the block, the title on bestseller lists, glowing reviews in the paper, the whole thing. But it's not clicking for me. I'm still not writing."

"I got really good at that too," Chloe said. "I realized, as emotionally involved as I was getting with the idea, a tiny part of me in the back of my mind still didn't see it. This little nugget in my brain was still focused on how it couldn't happen. No money, no time, the ridiculous odds of finding an agent willing to take it on, the even more ridiculous odds of finding a publisher interested in it, the whole self-publishing argument and wondering if that should be my approach, on and on. You think about any of that?"

Frank nodded. "All of it. I try to put it aside, but I just don't see how. Those are the nuts and bolts of the entire project. Of course they should be taken into consideration."

"Ah, then we're stuck on the same thing. Frank, you're so concerned with the outside variables that you're allowing them to dictate your inner self. Your thoughts, emotions, even your decisions are being affected by the outward, negative hypotheticals.

"In Unstuck terms, you're still subservient to outside influences instead of the true cause. It's the inner you, Frank. It's you. Your inner self. The cause of your behavior you are stuck on, your inability to write, is inside you. Your secret belief that it can't be done. Same as me, not so long ago."

Frank leaned back, clasping his hands atop his bare head. "What do I do?"

"I'll tell you what worked for me. I did the lesson two exercise every week. I made a list of nonproductive activities and a list of productive activities. I shredded the list of nonproductive activities, and I practiced the visualization exercise from lesson three. As I progressed and repeated the process, those outside variables faded into the background. That persistent nugget of negativity shrunk and fell silent. It didn't matter what those outside variables were, because emotionally, I had already achieved my goal. I *already was* the published author. My writing had already changed the world."

Finishing with some notes he'd been scribbling, Frank stared at the page before glancing up at the camera. "You should be an ambassador of Unstuck or something. You not only understand this, you understand me."

Chloe scoffed. "I haven't even finished it yet. I'm sure Sarah has plenty of help."

"Well, you should talk to her about it. I bet she'd let you write some articles and stuff for the website. Live seminars and webinars too. Even Sarah was a mentee at one point, right? Now she's at the top."

"We'll see," Chloe said. "I have to admit, I would like to write about the program. But it's too early for any of that. I'll let the retreat soak in and see how things look in a few months."

A muffled crash sounded somewhere off camera, followed by Claire yelling and the barking of what must have been the world's smallest dog. Chloe heard Claire say something about an armoire and "my good plates."

Frank groaned. "Ugh, she had to have a Morkie. Thing's only four months old and he's already wreaking havoc."

Chloe laughed, picturing Frank holding a little Morkie puppy. "Aw, what's his name?"

"Duke," Frank said, puffing up with pride.

"You . . . named him Duke?"

"Yeah, after John Wayne. What's wrong with that?"

"Nothing!" Chloe assured him. "Nothing at all. Just kinda tiny." She bit her lip to keep from laughing.

Claire hollered for Frank as Duke kept barking.

"I better go," Frank said. "Thanks for the talk. I'm gonna work with this."

"Anytime. Wait until we talk about our conversation this morning. It touches on all this in some new and interesting ways. It'll really help, so just keep going."

"Really? That's great. I'll keep plugging away."

"Awesome." Chloe put on her best John Wayne voice. "Adios, pilgrim."

"Ha ha, very funny," Frank said, squinting at her as Claire shouted for him again. "I'm coming, I said! Hang on a darn—"

The screen went black as Frank hung up, and Chloe burst into laughter.

*   *   *

An hour later, Chloe received a text from Sarah, and they met at the resort's boutique. A small, gleaming shop with austere lines and lavender walls, it oozed refinement and exclusivity. Chloe marveled at the athletic wear and resort fashion lining the inlaid wall displays, as well as the elegant display cases with their high-end sunglasses and other items.

"Now," Sarah said, "let's get you outfitted for the week!"

"Yeah, about that," Chloe said, feeling a bit awkward. "I am feeling I belong here and everything, and I'm doing pretty darn well careerwise, but if the merchandise doesn't have a price tag, I'm sure I can't afford it."

Sarah chuckled. "Don't worry about any of that. Today is on me. And to make you feel more comfortable, I have no choice but to get myself a few things as well."

Chloe swallowed a laugh, trying not to disturb the serenity of the shop and draw the ire of the runway model behind the counter, who appeared to be moonlighting as a high fashion sales clerk. "OK, I know better than to argue with you. But I have a feeling any one of these items is worth more than a month's rent."

"Not for long," Sarah said, picking out a summer dress and holding it up to Chloe. "I started your book last night, and I can say with even more certainty than ever, the days of things like this being out of your price range are numbered."

Chloe smirked at the presentiment and focused on the other news. "You started it already? Thoughts so far?"

"Nothing yet, other than the fact that it's better than I imagined. Given the emotion you evoke in your journalism, I knew fiction would be the ultimate playground for you. I had no idea it would grab me like it did, from the very first page. The way you write the mother and daughter has me wondering if you aren't drawing from real-life experience. I don't want you to say either way, if you don't want to. That's personal stuff."

"Thanks," Chloe said. "I borrowed from my own experience here and there, which was far less traumatic than the book. I'd say my past is pretty boring compared to the story, but I'm glad it came across in a profound way. A half dozen people have read it so far, but I've been dying for your thoughts on it. You get my writing in a way I can't explain."

"Just like you get the program in a way I can't explain," Sarah replied.

"Really?"

"Of course." Sarah held a sarong up to her. "How about this one?"

"Ooh, I love it."

Sarah draped it over an arm as she continued. "Since your football article, I've felt like I've known you all along. I can't explain that either. I knew enough to reach out and hope you'd respond. Your ability to Unstick yourself has been one of the most successful journeys I've ever seen.

"I know you'd like to chalk it up to coincidence, or timing, or good luck, or whatever else, but I've seen thousands of people from all walks of life make a run at getting Unstuck. Not all succeed, and those who do rarely do so as masterfully as you have.

"Now, reading your book, it's like listening to an old friend. You may marvel at the private jet and the resort and the tremendous success that allows such things, but the people who achieve that kind of success? They marvel at people like you."

Chloe stared at the stylish sunhat in her hands, blinking back tears. "I love you for saying that. It means more than you know. I've felt the same way as you. Ever since I first saw you onstage at the Hilton, I felt you were familiar, somehow.

What you were talking about didn't make a ton of sense at the time, no matter how interesting you made it. But the person onstage felt like an old friend to me. Someone I could trust. Someone I could believe in. Every time you tell me who I am, a piece of the old me dies, and a new part is born."

Sarah blinked back tears of her own as she grabbed Chloe's hand.

Chloe huffed a laugh. "I'm only now realizing how much I needed to hear those words. Especially from you."

The two embraced, sharing a quiet moment in a quiet shop, two old friends who had only recently met.

CHAPTER SIX

The Power of Praxis

Journaling on her terrace the next morning, Chloe thought back over the previous day, especially the afternoon she'd spent with Sarah. They'd hung out together for hours, sharing stories, talking about family and friends, and laughing about past relationships. It felt more as if they were catching up after a long time apart than cementing a new friendship. Sarah felt like the big sister she'd never had. The best friend she'd always wanted.

After hitting a few more boutique shops, the pair had stopped by the Olivier Hair Salon. On an impulse, Chloe decided to try a new look and had several inches of her long, flowing hair trimmed. Her scalp was then treated with some sort of vitamin soak, and she was given a number of bottles and vials with instructions designed to help her maintain and grow healthier, more luxurious hair. Sarah loved the new look, and so did Chloe.

After that, they spent some time at the cabana pool before gathering with the other attendees for a short ride down the road for dinner. Sarah was treating them to a private tasting dinner at French Laundry, one of the most exclusive restaurants in the country.

As they unloaded from their limos, chef Thomas Keller was there to greet Sarah and the group. "Sarah, I'm thrilled you decided to bring this distinguished group to dine with us."

"The honor is all ours, chef. Thank you for giving us the restaurant exclusively tonight. I know closing to other customers at this time of year isn't the most convenient for you."

"It's our pleasure. We've worked to make this menu something special for your group, especially since it is such an eclectic one. Some are vegetarians and others lusty carnivores. I think you will find something for everyone."

As they entered the restaurant, Chloe saw a simple, elegant interior with soft lighting, natural wood, and clean lines. There was nothing to distract from the culinary experience.

As the group took their seats at a round table in the center of the room, Keller continued. "We don't have a standing menu, as such. We determine the evening's offerings based on what we see as the best our suppliers have on offer. From there, we exercise our creativity and innovation to make the most enjoyable dishes possible.

"Our vegetables come from several small organic farms, which don't mass-produce but take great care with each plant. Our dairy supplier is organic, with a very keen eye on quality feed and the avoidance of unnecessary hormones and other chemicals. We want you to experience this food the way God created it."

Seated at Chloe's right, Min clasped her hands together. "I've wanted to eat at this place since forever! I even took Thomas Keller's master class to see if I could introduce a few of his cooking techniques into my repertoire."

"Oh really? How did that go?" Chloe asked.

Min chuckled. "Let's just say he has an amazing technique cooking zucchini. I think I mastered that one."

Two waiters made their way around the table, offering either flat or bubbly mineral water. Another waiter brought fresh, warm, sliced baguettes.

"You will see several carafes of olive oil at the table," Keller said. "I'm an especially great fan of this particular brand, and I hope you will taste why. An award-winning filmmaker, the Tuscan Armando Manni, got so discouraged with the quality of the extra virgin olive oil he found that he developed his own and revolutionized how it is packaged. You see, olive oil can oxidize once it's opened, and that affects the flavor. Manni thought outside the box and created a bottle that blocks UV rays. His olive oil retains a fresh flavor I have found only in Italy. He only bottles twenty-five hundred liters a year, and French Laundry is honored to be one of his customers."

Everyone at the table was dipping their bread in the oil to taste the difference. Chloe felt her taste buds awaken in a way they never had before.

"Oh my, it's delicious," commented Sarah. "I never knew the story behind this."

Keller swelled with pride at the smiles and nods all around the table.

"Now, if you'll excuse me, I have work to do in the kitchen. Bon appétit!"

*   *   *

Chloe had to pace herself—each course of the tasting menu was more delicious than the previous. All agreed this was a fabulous way to end an amazing day.

Once they returned to the hotel, some of the group wanted to go for a nightcap. Chloe begged off, telling them she felt she just *had* to journal, being a writer and all. That got smiles all around and a few attagirls.

The next morning, after checking emails, she got ready for the meeting, opting for a loose-fitting cotton button-down with matching high-waisted trousers. Slipping on a new pair of sandals, she smiled as she looked herself over in the dressing room's full-length mirror. She hardly recognized herself.

She glanced at the long line of new clothes hanging in the nearby closet. She couldn't wait for an excuse to wear every outfit. Along with a few hats, more shoes, and a handbag or two, Sarah had also insisted on gifting her a pair of trendy sunglasses and a gorgeous watch that somehow showed off her wrist.

Sighing, Chloe was still torn about it all. She certainly felt less like a fish out of water with the new wardrobe, but she wondered if she'd ever be in a position to see such a shopping spree as a matter of course. She enjoyed looking nice, but her endgame wasn't to be an extravagant spender. She wanted to be as comfortable in her own skin as she was in an expensive outfit.

Choosing the larger Prada bag, big enough for her binder, laptop, and a few other items, she shook herself out of her self-talk moment. It was more important to focus on the thought behind Sarah's shopping gesture than on the cost of it.

Arriving at the Study, she chatted with Min and Ricardo over coffee while they waited for Sarah. Joyce suggested they move to the open terrace. It had plenty of seats and tables, and it was a beautiful morning without too much wind.

"Good morning!" Sarah greeted everyone as they finished settling in. "I hope you had a lovely first day, yesterday. I'm glad you could all make the dinner at French Laundry."

"It was amazing! Thank you so much for that," someone said.

"Yeah, I've read about that place for years, and never thought I'd get to eat there, much less in a private group," added Sidney.

"All networking should be this fun, and delicious!" Min smiled at the group.

Sarah laughed. "Amen to that! Now, today we're looking at our eighth principle toward Unstuckness. It's called the Power of Praxis. Aligning you with you so we all win. And while the dinner was certainly delicious, there are some great lessons there for us too. This conversation embraces belief and behavior, and it solidifies and expands upon a lot of what we've learned thus far. Only individuals whose beliefs are virtuous and in harmony with the greater good, and whose behavior is driven by their virtue, will emerge as leaders in our human journey. Did you notice that Thomas identified like-minded suppliers for his restaurant?"

Nods all around.

"He sources good meat and produce—even artisanal olive oil, all in line with his vision. He has found allies, and in the process, they all succeed.

"Belief and behavior. Being in sync with yourself is a key element of getting and staying Unstuck. Learning how to get out of your own way.

"Acceleration is the energy, the DNA, of the twenty-first century. Constant change. Dr. Christopher Hegarty, an international authority on mastering change, identified three concepts we need to understand. Knowing, habit, and praxis.

"Praxis is the integration of belief and behavior. Thomas believes quality ingredients yield quality food on the table. I think you'll agree that he succeeded there. Now you might think that one's beliefs are automatically integrated with one's behavior, but that's not the case. It's similar to one's actions and words. How many times has someone told you their thoughts or beliefs, only to then watch them behave in a way that goes completely against what they professed? If Thomas paid lip service to organic food and artisanal products but bought at a big-box store, his results would be different. Integrating belief and behavior is a conscious choice, and it takes practice. It takes habit.

"Analyze the reasons behind your various beliefs. It's really complicated. And scary. Did you know only one in a hundred thousand people changes their mind on anything over the age of twenty? Beliefs should be based on constant evaluation. Not so for most. Anything worth believing is worth reevaluating, because things change. Adapting your beliefs to keep up with knowledge and developments is vital." Sarah looked around the terrace. "If we got honest here, we would be amazed at the things we believe because we were told what to believe decades ago. Yet we never honestly reevaluated what we were told. Many of us have other beliefs that we've never incorporated into our behavior. We believe we can do certain things, but we don't act on those beliefs. We may think we're acting on them. Most often, we're not.

"Take a look at our friendly Stickperson in your fancy journal. This illustrates the integration process, which can only take place through constant, spaced repetition and emotional impact. It goes back to the conscious and subconscious mind. We have belief in our educated mind, based on logic and our senses, and we have belief on a subconscious level, which controls our behavior and is part of our paradigm.

"Integration starts at the top of the Stickperson and works its way down. Analyze and adjust your beliefs consciously through repetitive practice. Internalize your reevaluated beliefs, which become absorbed by your subconscious, creating an emotional connection.

"The new beliefs manifest through your habits and behaviors. Remember, emotion is another word for vibration. The conscious thoughts about our beliefs, when internalized, set up your vibration, and this vibration is released into the world through your actions." Sarah paused for a moment and shivered. She ran her hand up and down the back of her neck and smiled at the group sheepishly. "I'm sorry. Whenever I get close to this conversation, I feel the vibration in every part of my body. The hair stands up on the back of my neck."

Everyone ran their hand across their neck as she continued. "Action causes reaction, which is the universe sending back that vibration in kind, in the form of the results of your new belief." She paused, her voice going soft. "It may be the closest to God you will ever come in this lifetime.

"As you can see, the individual and team exercise section for this conversation in your journal is extensive. You're going to come upon some fascinating insights that may blow your mind wide open. By describing your current beliefs about things like financial stability and your relationships, then comparing them to descriptions of the same after having imagined that you've already created what you want, lightbulbs will go on. You will see where your beliefs need adjustment, which beliefs you don't hold as dearly as you thought you did, and how to better internalize them and make that emotional impact on your subconscious.

"As you can imagine, the Three R's are going to come in clutch, here. To this day, I still perform this exercise at least a few times a year. Get familiar with it, because it's a remarkably effective practice in self-evaluation and maintenance."

As the group turned pages and jotted notes in their binders, Tom raised his hand. "This is amazing, because Sidney here is having a hard time with belief regarding our latest project."

Sarah pointed at the couple, excited. "Yes, this is perfect. I remember you telling me about this. If you like, share your story with us so we have some context, and we'll get a look at a real-life example of how praxis can help."

Sidney smiled at her husband, giving him the go-ahead. Tom turned to the group and continued. "Sidney and I met in college. After getting our degrees in software engineering, we spent several years at various firms before founding our own small company. The goal was to use our careers to fund our true passions. Sid's a musician, and I'm an artist. Fast-forward a few more years, and we've partnered with some great people to combine technology with the arts.

"We're working on augmented reality and virtual reality technology for museums and concerts. Imagine going to the Louvre and being handed a sleek pair of glasses. As you browse the exhibits, information pops up that tells you more about the art, but it pops up in a way that fits organically with your surroundings, like a small paragraph appears on the wall next to a painting.

"You can also choose a particular tour, and your display will be populated with a number of pieces. You'll then look around, and lighted paths will appear on the floor, directing you through the tour while providing specific information on the collection, including stats like tour duration, walking distance, highlighted artists and pieces, and so on.

"The other thing we're going for is virtual reality for symphonies and orchestras. We can bring the arts to young people around the world with this. Using existing VR hardware commonly used for gaming, we're putting together a library of events that can be viewed in VR, making it feel like you're really in the concert hall. This can be expanded to musicals, plays, all kinds of things. Someday we may even be able to do it with live streaming events."

There was a buzz in the room. "I would so buy that," someone whispered.

"It's exciting, but a slow process. Lots of moving parts. This stuff isn't easy, and even when we do move beyond testing and release it to the public, we have sales and marketing hurdles to overcome." He gestured toward Sidney. "We've both been at this for a few years now, and Sidney is still all about it. She definitely wants to see this succeed. But sometimes her actions speak differently. It's as if her heart isn't in it anymore. At least, not to the degree it used to be."

Sidney nodded. "It's hard to explain. I know we'll make it work, I know this is worth bringing to the world, but I think it might be like what we have been talking about. I don't *believe* it the way I need to believe it. It feels more like I'm just pretending to believe."

"Pretty great and gritty example," Sarah said. "Thank you both for sharing that." She looked around at the group. "Any thoughts? What can Sidney and Tom do to solidify her belief?"

Chloe spoke up. "There's a quote in the journal from Napoleon Hill that reads, 'No one's ready for a thing until they believe that they can acquire it. The state of mind must be belief, and not mere hope or wish.'

"It sounds like it could be an emotional disconnect," Chloe said. "Like Sidney said, she 'knows' the project will work, so her conscious mind is onboard. But the internalization isn't taking place." She paused, considering the quote she'd just read. "Napoleon's quote reminds me of another line I heard somewhere, years ago— 'some things must first be believed to be seen.'"

The group paused, many glancing at each other in surprise.

"Wow, that is a punch to the gut," Sidney said. "I had always seen belief like a harder version of hope or wish. It's not at all. It's a state of mind that has you living inside the thing you're believing. This is mind-blowing. It feels more real than the chair I'm sitting on."

"Brilliant," Sarah said. "That is just brilliant. And I've never heard that line before. You can't go beyond where you *believe* you can go. You must believe, first and foremost. The internalization, the emotional connection, and the subsequent results will follow. The exercises will help with that process. The results will be seen once they're believed." She gave Chloe a smile. "Good stuff, Chloe."

The group murmured their agreement as Sarah wrapped up. "All right, let's break out into groups and give these lessons a go, shall we? Then I say we hit the spa."

CHAPTER SEVEN

The Magic Word

Journaling once more at her bungalow balcony Wednesday morning, Chloe reviewed the previous day. It was a fascinating lesson, and she planned to incorporate it into her ongoing practice regimen. Just like on Monday, the group packed up around lunchtime and decided to try the resort's sushi bar. After that, Sarah, Chloe, and a couple others spent a few hours at the spa.

Chloe had never been pampered like that in her life. Manicure, pedicure, facial, Reiki massage, complete with a swag bag of exotic creams and moisturizers that would take her months to use up.

Sarah was already halfway done with her book. Huddled together, the two talked about the story, the publishing industry, and various writing projects they were each involved with. *Sunset at Whisper Creek* took place on a horse ranch, leading the two to discover their mutual love for horses and riding. Chloe began looking forward to these moments with Sarah as much as she did the lessons. She didn't know if Sarah would have time every day, but she hoped so.

Chloe brought Sarah up to speed on Frank, mentioning how she was coaching him on the early lessons, hoping it was OK for her to do so. Sarah was ecstatic that Frank had taken to Unstuck, figuring he was too hard-boiled for it. She loved the idea of a series of articles about the nature of success. Even more, she relished the fact that Chloe was coaching Frank, which gave Chloe a bit of needed courage.

As she put the finishing touches on her last journal entry, a group email came through from Sarah. She was inviting everyone to the Wine Center, telling them to get ready to enjoy some fine wine, with a curated tasting and wine pairing. They'd have a sommelier to teach them all about why Napa was famous for its wine. For the adventurous ones, there would even be a surprise field trip. She also recommended they either bring a pair of shorts or their bathing suits.

Excited, Chloe changed into a new outfit from the boutique, a cream sleeveless dress with a matching cotton cardigan thrown over her shoulders. With her favorite new sandals, a sleek wide-brimmed hat, and her new sunglasses, she was ready to go. Figuring that the bathing suit note meant swimming later, she put her new one-piece in her bag, along with her sunscreen.

When she got to the Wine Center, she saw a stylish yet simple room, with oak tables set in rows facing a speaker's podium in front. Each place had a line of wineglasses for red, white, and bubbly, plus a normal dinner place setting. Like the rest of the resort, the room had a bright, airy, natural feel. The French doors opened out onto a flagstone terrace, bordered by a hedge of green.

"This is more like it!" Sarah said, setting up her binder at the front of the room. "Just so you know, our next four topics are a bit more compact compared to the expansive lessons we've covered so far, but that doesn't mean they're any less profound. In fact, this next one has the power to change your results faster and more dramatically than anything else.

"After seeing how you've done so far, and after talking with many of you yesterday, I feel confident in saying that we're a little ahead of schedule. This leads me to believe that we'll gain even more ground over the next few days, so I think we're going to tackle the final two lessons on Friday, giving us all of Saturday and Sunday to let everything sink in and have one last hurrah before the retreat comes to a close. We may even have a surprise planned for you, but we'll have to see."

The group was all smiles, happy to see they were making good progress. And the hint of a surprise made them even more excited.

"So," Sarah continued, "we're meeting here because how can you come to wine country and not have a wine tasting?"

The group laughed.

"But this also helps illustrate our next topic. What does that next topic have to teach us? According to our journals, it's titled The Magic Word. The magic of attitude. And how do you like this? What do we see at the top here, but another quote from that brilliant young woman, Sarah Garner!"

The group chuckled as she read the quote. "'Genius is revealed through *attitude*. It is a *decision* that you can do well at what you were designed to do. Bring your gift to the surface, and become who you were meant to be. The brilliance of your gift is always seen more clearly by others than it is understood by you.'

"Did you know that the word *genius* was created to describe the spirit that arises from one's unique and innate ability at birth? It's a brilliant word. You are all geniuses in this room because we see you through the exercise of your God-given passion. You are so unique! I feel all of your vibrations right now." Sarah stopped for a moment and looked down. "You are overwhelming to me. I can hardly bear it."

Sarah looked up again at the group and continued. "We hear the word *attitude* all the time, since we were kids. It's one of the most misunderstood terms out there. A dozen people will get you a dozen definitions. How often are we told to improve our attitude? The fact is that attitude isn't governed by the external world.

"We are in control of our attitude. Attitude is the composite of your thoughts, feelings, and actions. It goes back to the mind-body connection and the relationship between your conscious and subconscious mind.

"Our trusty Stickperson joins us once again as we take a look at these three ingredients— thoughts, feelings, and actions.

"First up, thought. As we take in the world around us, this external, creative power is neither positive nor negative. It just *is*. At the point that we take in stimuli, the process of attitude begins. Say someone has shared some incredibly negative news with you. Your conscious mind has the ability to accept or reject any idea that comes its way, whether it originated in the external world or even inside yourself. If you reject it—meaning, if you choose not to internalize it—then it has no effect on your emotions or your body.

"The subconscious mind, however, what the early Greeks referred to as the heart of a person, distinct from the actual organ, is completely subjective. It doesn't differentiate between positive or negative. It accepts whatever's impressed upon it, without question. It is the nature of the idea you accept consciously, allowing it to be impressed upon the subconscious, that dictates your vibration of the emotion you express through your body, in the form of actions and behavior. Your higher intellectual faculties allow you to filter the ideas you allow in. The same at an intuitive level. Remember, *feeling* is just the word we use to describe the conscious recognition of vibration. So when those around you are putting out negative vibrations, you can 'feel' it. Learn to trust your intuition.

"This brings us to the third and final ingredient: actions. This, of course, is the purview of the body—working together, the conscious and subconscious mind harmonize to use the body to express themselves. When the mind is conflicted, conflicted behavior follows. Projects are started and never finished. Contradictory language and behavior are presented.

"When the conscious and subconscious are in harmony, ordered behavior follows. Precise language, focused productivity, steadfast accomplishment—all the things we tell ourselves are good things.

"Now take a look at these bottles of wine at the front. All were made under basically the same conditions. Yet each is different, with a different flavor, different attributes, as we'll taste in a bit. These bottles exist because in different circumstances, some winemaker brought his or her talent to the table and saw something others did not. One might say, each of these bottles has its own attitude, which reflects the person who made it. Each wine has subtle nuances, which an educated palate will discern.

"When we bring thought, feelings, and action together, we have a composite of one's attitude. Attitude is shaped by the nature of the ideas that your conscious mind allows in, the subsequent emotions impressed upon the subconscious, and the expression of those emotions in the form of actions.

"It all starts with governing your conscious mind. In this way, it is you who governs your attitude, not the whims of the external world.

"This lesson is a straightforward one, but incredibly impactful. Even more than most other lessons, I encourage you to revisit it often with the Three R's. You'll be surprised at all the nuance you uncover. The exercises are designed to walk you through the process of understanding and governing your attitude, namely by helping you decide if negative situations you're in are governing you or the other way around, and what to do from there. And that's it! Questions? Comments?"

Lisa raised her hand.

"Lisa! Go ahead."

Barely into her forties, Lisa Beaumont owned Gaia Electric Limited, the parent company of the world-renowned electric vehicle manufacturer, Gaia Automobiles. As renewable energy continued its push past fossil energy, her company was at the forefront of the industry. Her cars were synonymous with electric vehicles, and they could be found in every developed country in the world, their numbers increasing with each passing year.

Out of all the group's members, Lisa needed no introduction. The group perked up at her involvement. Although friendly and relaxed, she was quiet and reserved, so it was rare to hear her speak at any length.

"Thank you, Sarah. Two years ago, we introduced Unstuck at several of our locations, and the response was so positive that I had to see for myself when Sarah came to our city last year. I was thrilled to get an invite to this wonderful retreat after beginning the Unstuck journey. I've decided this week that I'm going to recommend to the board we roll out Unstuck company-wide. What you've touched on today is one of the many reasons why.

"As you can imagine, Gaia has many offices, factories, dealerships, and R&D labs around the world, all with their own leadership. It often feels like walking a tightrope through a complex web of social and political chaos. Between government regulations, international laws, victories and set-backs with research and development, and fierce competition from the fossil industry and other leaders in the EV space, it's an understatement to say that emotions run high. We've implemented several programs and resources to mitigate negative factors like work stress, poor management, and team conflicts, all to varying degrees of success. Much of it seems to come down to attitude.

"I have a number of executive teams in various countries who, at every opportunity, seem to react poorly to setbacks and bad news. It's part of their job, like any other, to work toward a resolution to negative issues. My question is, how does one manage this when one doesn't have the option to reject or ignore negative input from the external world?"

"And that, ladies and gentleman, is a five-star question," Sarah said. "What do we think, everyone? Any thoughts?"

The group looked around at each other, silent.

"I got nothing," Min said. "That's a real pickle."

Chuckles rippled across the room as others agreed.

Chloe raised her hand.

"Go ahead, Chloe," Sarah said.

"Well, thinking through our conversation, it looks like it's a little more nuanced that just the accept, reject, ignore option for the conscious mind. Part of resolving conflicts, especially in a team setting, is about learning how to think differently about what's going on. Figuring out how to look at the negative situation from a different angle to come up with a positive solution.

"It's almost like . . . I don't know. If the nature of the idea dictates the emotion impressed upon the subconscious, then use the conscious mind to change the nature of the idea. A simple example would be looking at a problem not as a problem, but as a challenge. It changes the tenor of the situation, allowing you to cultivate a more positive attitude by looking at the negative in a positive way. It all leads back to the importance of governing the conscious mind. We can do more than control what we let in. We can control how we *perceive* what we let in."

"Whoa," Min said. "Girl, you are on fire!"

The group laughed, followed by a smattering of applause.

"She really is!" Sarah said. "She is also absolutely right." Sarah smiled at Chloe and nodded. "Good stuff."

"Why don't we ask our sommelier, Claude, to introduce us to the first wine, and put Lisa's problem through our paces. We'll see what develops and take a few more examples from the group. The majority of you are interested in utilizing the program in the team and family setting, so this is a great opportunity to see how those kinds of conversations can go. And if all else fails, we'll see what Chloe charges for consultation!"

The group broke into laughter as Claude moved to the podium.

Sarah threw her arm around Chloe's shoulder and squeezed. "You so belong here," she whispered as they focused their attention on the tasting.

CHAPTER EIGHT

The Most Valuable Person

After the wine tasting with tapas, the group broke off into twos and threes to pursue various plans. Some headed to the tennis courts or the gym, others took off for a hike around the grounds. A handful of others decided on nine holes at a nearby golf club with the Meadowood pro.

A few were curious what extra surprise Sarah had in store for them and stuck around after the session. Claude was in on it—that was for sure. He had a secret grin, and when Sarah gave him the signal, he got the attention of those remaining.

"We have a little surprise for you," he shared. "One of our neighbors hails from a particularly famous wine-making region of Italy, and he loves doing things the old way, even if it's just for show these days. He has invited you over to his vine-yard to help him, if you're up for it."

Chloe looked at Min, who was practically bouncing in her seat. While Chloe did have her heart set on hanging out at the resort, this sounded like a once-in-a-lifetime opportunity. So she decided to join Min and two others.

As Claude ushered them to a waiting limo, Sarah made her apologies that she wouldn't be able to join them and asked them to have fun in her stead. Given the news that Lisa wanted to implement Unstuck across her entire company, Chloe wasn't surprised that Sarah had to spend the afternoon with the industry leader to hash out the details. She imagined the development was quite the boon for Sarah and the PG Insti-tute. However many certified consultants Sarah had on hand, she'd likely have to train a small army to meet the demands of a partnership that size. Chloe smiled. She couldn't have been hap-pier for Sarah.

Claude wouldn't let on what the big surprise was, but he did make sure that each of them had either shorts or their bathing suits with them before they departed. It was only minutes later when the limo pulled up to an ornate stone gate.

The sommelier entered a code, and the limo proceeded down a tree-lined driveway. Tall eucalyptus trees stood at attention on each side of the drive, giving the whole place an Old World vibe. Chloe was dying to find out exactly what this surprise really was.

At the end of the lane, the limo pulled into a circular drive. The driver hopped out to open the door, and the group found themselves in front of an elegant, well-cared-for wooden barn.

"Right this way," Claude said as he ushered them into the cool darkness of the barn.

They rounded a corner and there sat a big wooden vat. An older gentleman entered the room—and *gentleman* described him perfectly, thought Chloe. He had the air of a European duke or something.

"My guests! At last! You are Sarah's friends, yes?" They all nodded. "Sarah, she is a smart cookie. Any friend of Sarah's is a friend of mine, as you say here in America. Let me introduce myself. I understand this has been a mysterious surprise for you. My name is Vittorio Lombardo, and yes, my family is from the Lombardy region, hence the name. We have been winemakers for many generations, but alas, I was not the oldest son, so I did not inherit the family land—only the love of making great wine."

Chloe looked around the room as he spoke. Everywhere were classic wooden implements, not the steel ones in use today.

"Ah, young lady, you see my tools, yes?"

"Yes indeed. They look well loved."

"Very perceptive of you. You must be the writer Sarah told me about."

Chloe blushed.

"Aha! You are! See, I may be old, but I can still see beauty around me. Now, back to my story here. I came to this valley over forty years ago, when the only people making wine were not careful with what they were doing. The wine was not so good. So I saw an opportunity!"

He went to a small fridge under one of the worn wooden counters and pulled out a bottle of prosecco.

"This, my friends, is made with my grapes. I grow several varieties and sell them to the vineyards."

"How do you know which to grow?" asked Min.

"The soil tells me what it wants to do. Each area has its own charm, or desire. I just listen."

Claude interjected. "Vittorio supplies grapes to some of the major vineyards in the area, but he's too modest to brag. So I will. His champagne grapes are the best in the country."

"Thank you, my friend. This is why I want to share this bottle with you while you help me prepare next year's bottling."

Chloe's eyes opened wide. "We're going to help you make your wine?!"

Vittorio chuckled. "In a manner of speaking, yes. You see this wooden vat in front of you?"

All nodded.

"I want you to participate in a time-honored tradition—the stomping of the grapes."

The group started laughing.

"Like in *I Love Lucy*!" cried Min.

Vittorio laughed. "Not exactly, but I hope it will be fun. This is a tradition not many honor anymore. I don't do this with all the grapes—just the first of the harvest. And this, my friends, is the first."

At that, the rear barn door opened, and a tractor pulling a wagon filled with white champagne grapes pulled up to the vat. Chloe and the group were spellbound.

Vittorio broke the spell. "I hope you brought shorts or other clothes you won't mind getting wet. Since these are white grapes, I don't think they will hurt your clothes. Would anyone like to change?"

Everyone's hands went up. As Vittorio ushered them to the restrooms beyond the tasting room, the farmhand started filling the vat with grapes. By the time Chloe and the others returned, the grapes were about three feet deep in the vat.

Chloe laughed. She never in a million years thought she'd get to do this. She couldn't wait to jump in and release the last of the tension she'd been feeling about everything on her plate.

"Before you start, just a few words of advice. Have fun. And once you really get going, it can get slippery, so be careful. Now, who's the first in?"

Chloe raised her hand.

"All right, young lady writer, let's go." He offered her his arm and helped her climb over the top of the vat. As she sank down into the grapes, she could feel them squishing between her toes. She started laughing again.

"This is why I keep this tradition alive. For joy. Who's next?"

*   *   *

The following morning, Chloe reviewed what she'd written after returning from the stomping of the grapes. She'd laughed all afternoon, then returned to her aerie overlooking the vineyards, feeling completely relaxed. The soothing atmosphere of the place allowed her to slip into her writing zone. The surroundings fell away, the words poured forth from her fingertips with remarkable ease, and several hours flew by in a matter of minutes.

Reviewing the four thousand words in front of her now, she could safely say it had been one of the most productive writing sessions in recent memory. Nearly everything was worth keeping and would need minimal self-editing before submission. Frank and the brass were going to love it. Sipping her coffee, she reveled in the feeling. There was nothing quite like the euphoric high of finishing a piece of writing.

After getting ready and rushing off to the Study, she arrived just as Sarah was getting started. They gave each other a smile as Chloe slipped into a leather armchair near the fireplace.

"Happy Thursday, everyone!" Sarah said. "How are we feeling today?"

The group responded with energy and excitement, ready for another conversation.

"Wonderful to hear," Sarah continued. "Today, we're discussing lesson ten, titled The Most Valuable Player. Given that you're all accomplished leaders, it should come as no surprise to you that the MVP is, of course, the leader. As Larry Wilson said, 'A leader is a person who has people following them because they want to.'

"If the final three lessons of the program were to have a theme, leadership would be it. We'll be discussing various aspects of the topic for the remainder of our time together, so those of you in a team environment will learn a lot in our discussions. It is every bit as meaningful for the individual as well. The leadership we're talking about extends beyond the workplace. It applies to your whole life journey.

"Being an effective leader is a complex and delicate matter, requiring you to be rigid yet flexible, independent yet collaborative. Unstuck approaches leadership from an eminently human perspective. Healthy relationships with your people, from the executive team to the part-time employee, are paramount to your success and the success of your company or community. Fostering teamwork and putting yourself out there as an example enables people to *want* to follow you.

"And that starts by being a strong originator. It is up to you to establish and maintain a consistent idea, a steadfast vision, that your team can rally behind in order for everybody to move forward as one. That often requires you to reject ideas, both your own and those of others, that detract from that vision.

"At the same time, good ideas and the creativity to work them through require a commitment to new possibilities, especially those that fit within the confines of your vision. Successful collaboration requires a diversity of thinking. It is the new diversity, being able to work alongside people who think differently than you do. Knowing when to be the originator of an idea and when to be the collaborator of diverse thinking is the sign of a twenty-first century leader.

"You'll face resistance for your efforts, to be sure. That's an inevitable part of it. But what separates you from those around you is that unlike them, you are being led from within. Others don't see what you see, and sometimes there is pushback. Nevertheless, keep people around you who think differently than you. They can be priceless.

"The effective leader is open to the moment. They are active listeners, ever observant, they withhold ego, and they're interested in creation, not competition. When outside ideas are weighed and found superior, they incorporate them willingly and openly, crediting the team member or members responsible and thus fostering the kind of team that *wants* to give their best.

"This discussion is about more than evaluating what makes an effective leader. It's about helping your team members become effective leaders in their own right.

"That's how we all started, right? To be an effective team leader, your people must first focus on becoming effective team members. A leader can't very well lead if they don't have the experience of being an effective teammate.

"The exercises in this lesson are designed to help you elevate your leadership. They also allow teams to understand their dynamic and learn how to come together properly and move forward together. The team aspect has been found to be incredibly effective at healing and improving teams, making all the exercises ripe for constant rereading, rethinking, and rewriting. Any questions before we get into the exercise portion?"

"I have one," Min said, raising her hand. "I've got several labs around the country focused on specific projects, the largest of which is research and development of algal bioplastics. There's a definite hierarchy, as in any business, and like Lisa's situation, emotions often run high. To me, most of the emotion is ego-related. Academics are famous for this, even more so than business types. Frankly, I'm sick of it. It's disruptive, it erodes teamwork, and it saps hard-won resources.

"We're trying to solve the global plastics crisis, but my leaders are more interested in putting their workers in their place, and the workers are more interested in one-upping their leaders. More than once, a lab has devolved into a quagmire of petty office politics, grinding progress to a halt and jeopardizing our timeline and our funding.

"My default response has been to strong-arm the situation and force everyone back on track, but it never works. I'm just pounding a square peg into a round hole. It doesn't last. Even disciplinary measures and transfers don't work. Is there ever a point where a team is too far gone?"

Sarah shook her head. "Heavyweight questions this week. Teams are never too far gone. Your most valuable assets are your employees, each one. The figure I have heard is the replacement value of each employee is two and half times their latest annual salary." Someone let out a low whistle. "Play with *that* number in your head. We want to make sure we have used every resource available to turn those teams around.

"Your workers need as much help as your leaders. Your teams need to *want* to follow their leaders. We need them to *want* to be effective teammates. We need to understand why they aren't working effectively as a team. It's always about asking the right questions. You can't come up with the right answers if you aren't asking the right questions.

"As for your leaders, you need to evaluate what they're doing right and what needs to be changed. Along the way, everyone needs a thoughtful, evocative reminder of why they joined the organization in the first place. They sound like passionate people, so we need to tap into that passion and get them excited about their goals again.

"We can talk more about it in private, but I recommend we send a few consultants your way to get the lay of the land. After some interviews and a good look around, they'll be able to come up with the questions designed to get your labs back on track. If I were to hazard a guess, I'd say a local three-day retreat to go over Unstuck would help give everyone the perspective they need. Let them step back, take a breath, and find their desire for change."

Min smiled as she jotted some notes. "That sounds awesome, thanks."

"All right everyone," Sarah said, "let's run through these exercises so we can lead each other to the pool and some type of drink with a fancy umbrella."

CHAPTER NINE

INCREASE AND MAGNIFICATION

The rest of Thursday flew by in a blur. After lunch, Chloe got caught up in conversation with Min, Lisa, and Ricardo, the social media magnate. The three of them talked about the program and their respective fields, and shared stories about friends and family. That led to dinner at the Terrace Bar with the majority of the group, followed by a glass of wine in the Study, seated around the fireplace, which had a fire going to ward off the chill that evening. Chloe solidified some wonderful network connections that were bound to lead to something fun and interesting in the future. She even made a few new friends.

Finishing her Friday morning journal entry on her terrace, she drank a quick spinach and fruit smoothie for breakfast, donned a new out-fit of breezy cotton with a tropical pattern, and made her way back to the Study. Sarah arrived shortly after, and once everyone settled in, they began the final meeting of the week.

"Happy Friday, ladies and gentlemen," Sarah said. "Here we are, our last meeting. As I men-tioned, the final two lessons continue the topic of leadership, and since we're ahead of schedule and have a number of fun things planned for the week-end, it's the perfect time to have a double feature!

"Lesson eleven is titled 'Leaving Everyone with the Impression of Increase: The Number One Key to Success.' Though we're looking at it through the lens of leadership, it still applies to everyone, making it an effective tool for those working under you.

"The book and movie *The Secret* revealed a particular reality to its worldwide audience of millions. Every aspect of our lives is governed by the natural laws of the universe. In the movie, President John F. Kennedy asked Dr. Wernher von Braun, the father of the space program, what it would take to put a man on the moon.

"Dr. von Braun had a simple answer: 'The will to do it.'

"Confident and direct. Why? Because Dr. von Braun understood the laws involved, and he knew that by working in harmony with them, you can accomplish anything. We won't be going over all the laws here, but we will be focusing on one in particular—the law of cause and effect.

"It will help you give some thought to the one thing we all have in common. We are sacred beings, and that sacredness is always seeking expansion and fuller expression. As Wallace Wattles said, 'The desire for increase is inherent in much of nature. It is a fundamental impulse of the universe. Many human activities are driven by the passion for increase. Beyond the necessities, we have been designed to acquire more—more clothes, better shelter, more luxury, more beauty, more knowledge, more pleasure. More life. It is a part of many of our gifts. Where increase of life ceases, dissolution, decay, and death set in. It's why so many age faster than those with the gift of increase.'

"By putting others first and leaving them with the sensation of increase, you're putting yourself in harmony with a universal law. Even those without the gift will find themselves inspired by the vibration they feel through you. They want to associate with you because they feel more alive.

"In the words of Jane Willhite, 'Givers gain.' By making the worlds of others larger, you elevate those around you. By making others and their increase a part of your paradigm, the universe responds in kind. Cause and effect.

"The universe is subjective. It receives and reacts, not differentiating between good and bad. We are connected to its energy. Action and reaction. That's why the Three R's are so important. By constantly improving our old paradigm, the program, and our lives, we improve what the universe bestows on us. Give abundance to all, wherever you go, and you will receive abundance in return. Make giving a habit, a part of your paradigm, and the impression of increase will touch everyone around you.

"The exercise for this lesson is simple. Choose one person from three different areas of your life and answer the questions provided. This will help you understand the increase mindset. And Min, I think this one especially might do wonders for your teams. Questions?"

Ricardo raised his hand. "Similar to Lisa and Min, my social media platform, Ding!, requires large teams headquartered throughout the world. Various leaders and teams report less generous approaches to their interaction, causing all manner of strife. It's not good for business, of course, but it's also not good for my people, no matter where they fall in the chain of command. I've been talking with Lisa, Min, and Chloe, and I'd also like to bring Unstuck to my company. I do see complications, however. Unfortunately, I envision certain leaders who would twist this and foster a culture of trade masked as generosity. How would I combat that?"

"Great question, Ricardo, thank you," Sarah said. "What do we think, everyone?"

"Whatcha got for us, Chloe?" Min said, prompting a round of laughter.

Chloe laughed as well, but her humor faded when she saw their expectant faces. She gave the question some thought. "Well, just like with Min, I doubt discipline or shuffling teams around would solve anything. That would be treating the symptoms instead of the cause. And I think *cause* is the key term here. What's prompting your leaders to prefer trade over generosity? What are they getting that isn't being provided through you and your company's generosity?

"If it's an ego thing, there are lessons for that. If it's due to a belief that it's the best way to satisfy their ambitions, there are lessons for that as well. To me, it sounds like they're lacking something—not an external deficit, but an internal one.

"I think a few rounds of interviews with certified consultants would help get to the bottom of it and provide these leaders with whatever it is they're missing. They're misbehaving because they don't see a better way. But you can give them one."

"Well put," Sarah said as the group nodded their agreement. "We find out the why, then we formulate the how. All right everyone, let's dig in before moving on to the final lesson. Joyce is rustling us up some coffee and finger sandwiches to help us push through to the end."

*   *   *

After a quick bite to eat while stretching their legs on the terrace, the group settled back in for lesson twelve.

"Our last conversation," Sarah said, handing out a thin paperback to each of the members. "It's called 'Magnifying the Mind.' It's the secret to increasing the power of your mind.

"There are no exercises at the end, but instead a set of principles and guidelines for a higher echelon of education, understanding, and prosperity. It's a jumping-off point that allows you to embrace humankind's desire for expansion and growth.

"When you get home, please take a peek at Price Pritchett's incredible book *You²*. It's a clever discussion about how to revolutionize the way you look at your performance when it comes to your goals and the results you want to see. Sometimes they come in structured, logical steps, and sometimes they come by leaps and bounds.

"It's true that there are exponential gains to be had, instead of only incremental progress. At first, this kind of multiplicative gain seems farfetched. You will have to set aside logic, which is not an easy thing to do. Given the current company, I think you're better at that than most.

"I bet when Ricardo began telling his friends and colleagues years ago that he was going to build the next global social media platform, they begged him to see reason, to think logically.

"When Lisa discussed her desire to revolutionize the auto industry, I'm sure she got strange looks. When Min went for grants and investment, talking about ridding the world of its plastics crisis and creating green solutions that would impact the global ecosystem, I bet many investors turned her away. The same with Tom and Sidney, and their marriage of technology and the arts.

"All of us require the suspension of logic at one point or another." She looked at Chloe. "Even when our main goal is simply to become someone we can be proud of.

"So it is with your next steps beyond Unstuck. All this is made easier by having trusted partners by your side. Fellow Unstuckers, who don't balk at your lofty goals and your plans to achieve them at an exponential pace. In fact, they help you with those goals, and in turn you help them with theirs. Leaders and innovators at this level understand each other in ways that others cannot. You have the ability to create a group paradigm, one that others would see as nonsensical, maybe even crazy. Ford, Einstein, the Wright brothers, they were seen as crazy too. Only after the fact is the impossible then deemed genius. This group knows that better than any I've ever been a part of.

"As I said, this lesson is more introduction than education. It's meant to show you that, as

Hamlet said to Horatio, 'There are more things in heaven and earth than are dreamt of in your philosophy.' The universe is infinite, as is our potential. Unstuck is only the beginning of your exploration of both.

"A final quote from Napoleon Hill:

When two or more people coordinate in a spirit of harmony,
and work toward a definite objective,
they place themselves in a position through that alliance to absorb power from the great universal storehouse of infinite intelligence.
It is a source to which the genius turns.
It is the source to which every leader turns.
It is the benefit that comes to all who mastermind following the mastermind principles.

"I think he got it right."

CHAPTER TEN
GOODBYES

The group remained in the Study past dinnertime, talking in earnest about Unstuck. Reconvening at Meadowood's restaurant for a late celebratory dinner, they moved on to the Terrace Bar for drinks and a hilarious few rounds of Celebrity.

On Saturday, Sarah invited everyone to join her at dawn. Coffee and breakfast smoothies were provided while they drove across miles and miles of farmland. Waiting for them in a random field were three hot-air balloons! Sarah had scheduled a balloon ride across the vistas of wine country. Chloe had never been in a balloon and was concerned she might get a little nauseous or fearful of the heights. Yet once the balloon took off, she was spellbound, enjoying every minute—especially the quiet.

At the end of the trip, Meadowood staff had set up a marvelous picnic featuring a long, low table surrounded by cushions and shade umbrellas, laden with the resort's freshest dishes and a selection of wines from their private cellar. With placeholders at each seat, the group found a large canvas gift bag personalized for each of them, filled with a selection from Meadowood's boutiques, including clothing, accessories, beauty products, a unique piece of jewelry, and a variety of gift cards for their next visit.

As the sun began to set, the group grew increasingly confident that the surprises were over, but Sarah had one more in store. Resort staff set up a small dais with folding chairs and two large, blank screens to the left and right. Shortly after, a string quartet made its way across the lawn and onto the impromptu stage. Cries went up among the group as they realized the woman with the cello was Sidney. No sooner did the news spread than Tom came around with a sleek pair of augmented-reality glasses for each of them. As the quartet warmed up, he gathered everyone close and gave them a quick tutorial on how to use them.

Chloe was floored when the quartet opened up with their first piece. The title appeared on one screen, and as the melodious notes filled the air, the second screen filled with flowing writing, giving brief facts about the music and its composer. Chloe pulled her glasses down, finding only blank screens next to the musicians. As the light began to fade with the setting sun, the AR glasses somehow adjusted the brightness of the script, making it easily readable. Even with the quartet's small stand lights and the two nearby bonfires lit by the staff, the AR experience remained consistent. One screen asked if she'd like to know more about the composer, and as Tom had instructed, she tapped the right corner of her glasses, where the bow met the frame, accepting the offer. An image of the composer appeared, with more information about them.

As the quartet flowed from one piece to the next, the AR experience grew more sophisticated, asking questions and providing options, taking each audience member on a fascinating journey of their own creation. Chloe understood how these experiences would change lives. The spectacle even drew other resort guests, prompting Tom and the group members to share their glasses and whisper excitedly with perfect strangers.

By the end of the concert, a crowd of fifty or more had gathered. Their cheers and applause filled the area as Sarah's party took the decorative flowers from the vases on the table and threw them at the quartet's feet. Sidney laughed as the quartet took their bows, then she motioned for Tom to join them. They waved to all as the crowd's appreciation echoed into the night.

*   *   *

The following morning, the group met for brunch at the Forum, Meadowood's casual restaurant. Though they had the rest of the day to enjoy the resort, many had a fair bit of travel ahead of them before reaching home, and they wanted to get things underway. After brunch, hugs and handshakes were everywhere as all said their goodbyes. They exchanged business cards, with everyone's info making its way to Chloe's hands.

They had all heard about her upcoming book. Lisa in particular wanted to read it, promising to shout the title from the rooftops and give it to all her friends and colleagues.

Ricardo did the same, mentioning that he'd feature her on Ding! to help spread the word to his one billion users and counting. He gave her his personal number and told her to call him when the book hit the preorder stage. They'd set up a marketing plan for her account. Giving her a wink, he said they'd get her title to number one on every list in the land. Chloe gave special good-byes to Tom and Sidney, as well as Min. With that, the week had come to an end.

Sarah mentioned to Chloe that she had business in L.A., and they could take her jet back home together. Chloe was glad to hear it, not wanting to say goodbye to her closest friend just yet. A few hours later, they were in the air, relaxing on the long sofa across from the TV.

"I finished your book," Sarah said.

"Really?"

"Yeah, three days ago."

"What?" Chloe said with a laugh. "When did you sleep?"

"I didn't, but it was worth it. The world has been waiting for your voice, Chloe. I hope you're ready for this. Your days of obscurity are over. Not even your publisher is going to be prepared for what's about to come."

"You think so?"

"I know so. We have a few months until pre-order, so I'd like to have a meeting with your publisher, if you'll allow it."

"Yeah, of course," Chloe said. "What for?"

"There's going to be a bottleneck. Soon after launch, demand for the book is going to outstrip whatever mechanisms Multmountain has in place. Once retailers start crying for copies, that demand is going to skyrocket. When we show them the backing you have, I think they'll be very interested in upping their investment in printing and logistics. We want to mitigate that bottleneck as much as we can. It could mean additional sales in the hundreds of thousands."

"Whoa. That's a lot of money."

Sarah laughed. "Not dollars. I'm talking copies sold. The revenue will be into the millions."

"Oh," Chloe breathed.

"See what I mean?"

Chloe nodded.

Sarah paused, a contemplative look on her face. "You remember how I said at the Hilton that I was tempted to have you come work for the institute?"

"Yeah."

"Well, I'm not sure that's the best idea. I think I have something better."

"Writing for the institute? I've been meaning to ask you about that."

"Is that something you'd like to do?"

"It is," Chloe said. "Nearly everything I'm writing, whether it's this nature of success series, other pieces for news outlets, or even my books, they all contain at least a hint of something I picked up from Unstuck. I've incorporated it into everything I do, my entire way of thinking. Even my way of storytelling. After this retreat, that's only going to become more evident. I'm only going to want to write about it more."

Sarah smiled. "That's very good news for me."

"I was even thinking maybe I could have the best of both worlds. Write for the institute while also writing fiction. What if we started an ongoing anthology series, from all kinds of members, telling their story in a fictional setting? It'd show real-world examples of how Unstuck changes lives. It'd be like word-of-mouth on an exponential scale."

"I love that idea," Sarah said. "While we're at it, we might as well start our own publishing company. But first thing's first. I don't think you should work for the institute. I think you should run it. I want you to take it over for me."

Chloe frowned, her mind blank. "What?"

"Look at this past week, Chloe. You have a gift for this stuff. I know writing is your passion. Clearly, so is leadership."

"But take it over? I don't even know what that means."

"You're helping Frank. You gave great coaching advice this week, and you did so every bit as articulately as I ever could. You're a natural inspiration."

Chloe looked out a window, into the blue expanse. "Speaking's not my favorite, though I could see myself getting into it, sure. But why take over?"

"You're a leader, Chloe. Not just any leader. This week, you took billionaires to school on ideas you'd only just been exposed to. Don't you see what that means? You're a leader *of leaders*."

Chloe met Sarah's gaze and held it. "But why won't you answer me? Why do I have to take over to do any of that?"

Sarah heaved a sigh. "Because I need to make sure my work is left in good hands."

Chloe's face grew dark as she searched Sarah's eyes. "Why would you have to do that?"

Sarah opened her mouth, then closed it. After a pause, she met Chloe's gaze. "They found three lumps a few weeks ago. Stage four. It exploded out of nowhere. It's aggressive."

Chloe gasped. She couldn't believe it. Sarah was in her fifties. She scooted closer to Sarah and wrapped her in a tight hug. "No, no, no. Tell me this isn't true. Tell me."

Sarah hugged her as they wept together. "I guess there's never a good time to die, is there?"

Chloe breathed hitched in her throat. "What are we going to do?"

Sarah kissed Chloe on the cheek. "We are going to do this together, if you're willing."

"I'm here," Chloe mumbled into her shoulder. "My sweet Sarah. I'm here."

Sarah blinked back tears. "I'll believe you when you accept my offer."

Chloe pulled away and nodded. "I'll do it."

"You will?"

"Yes. I'll take on your work."

Sarah smiled. "Did the cancer guilt you into it?"

Chloe nodded. "Maybe a little. Maybe a lot."

"I'll take it," Sarah said.

They held each other for a time, not saying anything.

"One way or another, we will get through this," Chloe said.

Sarah hugged her tight. "I believe you."

Milton Keynes UK
Ingram Content Group UK Ltd.
UKHW020714061224
3460UKWH00027B/241